Sumo Skills

Sumo Skills
Instructional Guide for Competitive Sumo

Thomas Zabel

Sumo Skills

Instructional Guide for Competitive Sumo

Copyright © 2014 Thomas Zabel

All rights reserved. No part of this publication may be used or reproduced, stored in a retrieval system, or transmitted in any form or by any means—electronic, mechanical, digital, photocopy, recording, or any other—except for brief quotations in printed reviews, without the prior permission of the publisher.

Publisher:

Ozumo Academy Publishing

310 County Rd 2740

Mico, TX 78056

Phone: 210-478-2267

mrsumo@ozumoacademy.com

www.ozumoacademy.com

ISBN: 978-0-9914086-0-3

Illustrations by Maggie Keller and Thomas Zabel

CONTENTS

ACKNOWLEDGEMENTS ix
FOREWORD xi
Chapter 1—SUMO HISTORY 1
    TYPICAL SUMO WORKOUT REGIMEN. 5
    WEIGHT DIVISIONS 6
Chapter 2—THE MAWASHI 9
    HOW TO FOLD 10
    HOW TO TIE 10
Chapter 3—THE REFEREE (GYOJI) AND JUDGES (SHINPAN) 15
    POSITIONING OF JUDGES 15
    PRELIMINARY ACTIONS 16
    STARTING THE MATCH. 17
    THE MATCH 18
    CHALLENGES BY THE SHINPAN: 21
    DIALOGUE OF THE GYOJI 22
Chapter 4—FUNDAMENTAL SUMO MOVEMENTS 23
    SONKYO 23
    CHIRICHOZU 24
    POSTURE OF CHUGOSHI 26
    ANGLES OF CHUGOSHI 26
    SHINKYAKU 27
    SHIKO 28
    KOSHIWARI 30
    SURIASHI (HAKOBIASHI). 31
    UKEMI 34
    MATAWARI (KAIKYAKU) 36
    TEPPO 37
    FROM SHIKIRI TO TACHIAI 38
Chapter 5—BASIC SKILLS 39
    INITIAL CHARGE (TACHIAI) 39
    INITIAL CHARGE (TACHIAI) STYLES. 41
    THRUST (TSUKI) TRAINING 45
    FORCE OUT (YORI) TRAINING 46
    DEFENSE (MAESABAKI) TRAINING 47

    ADDITIONAL SKILLS 49

Chapter 6 — TECHNIQUES 53
    INTRODUCTION TO TECHNIQUES 53
    KEY ELEMENTS 53
    GUIDE TO UNDERSTANDING JAPANESE TERMINOLOGY 55
    TECHNIQUE SIMILARITY LIST 56
    82 WINNING TECHNIQUES 58
    DEFAULT TECHNIQUES (HIWAZA) 59
    ADDITIONAL RULES 60
    PROHIBITED FOULS (KINJITE) 60
    MOST FREQUENTLY USED TECHNIQUES 61
    YORIKIRI 62
    YORITAOSHI 63
    OSHIDASHI 64
    OSHITAOSHI 65
    HATAKIKOMI 66
    HIKIOTOSHI 67
    TSUKIDASHI 68
    TSUKIOTOSHI 69
    UWATENAGE 70
    UWATEDASHINAGE 71
    SOTOGAKE 72
    UCHIGAKE 73
    KATASUKASHI 74
    KIMEDASHI 75
    KOTENAGE 76
    OKURIDASHI 77
    SHITATENAGE 78
    SUKUINAGE 79
    TSURIDASHI 80
    UTCHARI 81

Chapter 7 — COMMONLY USED TECHNIQUES 83
    ABISETAOSHI 84
    ASHITORI 85
    HIKKAKE 86
    KAINAHINERI 87

KAKENAGE	88
KEKAESHI	89
KETAGURI	90
KIMETAOSHI	91
KIRIKAESHI	92
KOMATASUKUI	93
KOSHINAGE	94
KOTEHINERI	95
KUBINAGE	96
MAKIOTOSHI	97
NICHONAGE	98
OKURIHIKIOTOSHI	99
OKURINAGE	100
OKURITAOSHI	101
OKURITSURIDASHI	102
SHITATEDASHINAGE	103
SHITATEHINERI	104
SOKUBIOTOSHI	105
SUSOHARAI	106
SUSOTORI	107
TOTTARI	108
TSUKITAOSHI	109
UCHIMUSO	110
USHIROMOTARE	111
UWATEHINERI	112
WARIDASHI	113
WATASHIKOMI	114
Chapter 8 — UNCOMMON TECHNIQUES	115
AMIUCHI	116
CHONGAKE	117
GASSHOHINERI	118
HARIMANAGE	119
KAWAZUGAKE	120
KOZUMATORI	121
KUBIHINERI	122
MITOKOROZEME	123

	NIMAIGERI	124
	OMATA	125
	OSAKATE	126
	SABAORI	127
	SOTOKOMATA	128
	SOTOMUSO	129
	TSUKAMINAGE	130
	TSURIOTOSHI	131
	YAGURANAGE	132
	YOBIMODOSHI	133
	ZUBUNERI	134

Chapter 9 — RARE TECHNIQUES 135
- IPPONZEOI 136
- IZORI 137
- KAKEZORI 138
- OKURIGAKE 139
- OKURITSURIOTOSHI 140
- SAKATOTTARI 141
- SHUMOKUZORI 142
- SOTOTASUKIZORI 143
- TASUKIZORI 144
- TOKKURINAGE 145
- TSUMATORI 146
- TSUTAEZORI 147

BIBLIOGRAPHY 149

ACKNOWLEDGEMENTS

With special thanks:

To Mr. "Blackie" Rokozu Sawagashira, who first got me into sumo as an athlete with the Misawa Air Base/City team. He worked with the American GIs from the base for many years and was always willing to share his culture with us. He was also instrumental in the award of my 1st degree black belt from Japan Sumo.

To Mr. Maeda and Mr. Machia, my Japanese coaches and trainers, always the encouragers. I was under their instruction for six years and they taught me the fundamentals of sumo that I hope to pass on to my students. I loved traveling with them to the local tournaments.

To the Misawa City Budokan (Martial Arts Center), where we did all of our sumo practicing. You are always very supportive of the American GIs.

To the local cities of Aomori, Towada, Hachinohe, Takko, Johoji, Sannohe, Nango, Katsuro, and others. The local residents always made me feel welcome and encouraged us to participate in their festivities with the pounding of the rice cakes, dancing, and, of course, their sumo tournaments.

To Chiyonofuji, whom I consider the greatest Yokozuna. When I first arrived in Japan in 1982 and started watching professional sumo, he was "the man" and was the person who most piqued my interest in sumo.

To Takamiyama, the first foreign-born rikishi to win the top division championship (1972). I had the privilege of meeting Jesse in 1988. He, along with Blackie, were instrumental in fostering cultural relations between the U.S. and Japan through sumo on the base at Misawa. He was my hero for being the first American role model in Japanese professional sumo.

To Konishiki, Akebono, and Musashimaru, three more American role models in professional sumo. I had the honor of meeting Saleva'a and Chad in Odate before a sumo exhibition (jungyo) where I delivered a couple ice chests full of American beef and hot dogs. All three of them inspired me to do the best I could on the dohyo and also to be a good example for America when I traveled to the local competitions.

To Katrina Watts for her review, suggestions, and endorsement of this manual.

And to my wife, Karen, who has supported me over the last 23 years while I pursued a passion in a uniquely different sport. Without her support, none of my accomplishments would have been possible. To quote a line from the movie Jerry Maguire, I don't know a better way to say it—Karen, "you complete me." You've made me a better person in all aspects of my life.

FOREWORD

Sumo Skills is an excellent manual for those involved in amateur sumo. As its full title states, it is an instructional guide for competitive sumo, which will prove of great value to coaches and athletes alike.

The explanations of the fundamental movements and basic skills are clear and easy to understand, with particularly helpful illustrations and diagrams. Information about the frequency of use added to the excellent explanations of the techniques is a good guide to where focus should be directed.

The explanation of the Japanese terms used by the gyoji is useful to audience and athlete alike.

Amateur sumo has progressed from being a Japanese sport to one practiced in over 80 countries, with their own local, national, and continental championships in addition to the annual Sumo World Championships and inclusion in the international multi-sport competitions, The World Games, and Sport Accord World Combat Games. However, in the world of amateur sumo, not everyone has a direct link to experienced coaches. This instructional guide sets everything out so clearly that it will be possible for athletes to work on their own to hone their skills between training sessions, and for coaches and administrators of the sport, explaining the rituals and practices of sumo will become much easier with this manual on hand.

I am certain that use of the *Sumo Skills Instructional Guide* will lead to a better understanding of sumo and significantly raise the standard of competition worldwide.

Katrina Watts
President, Australian Sumo Federation
International Sumo Federation Board Member
Former NHK Sumo Commentator

Chapter 1

SUMO HISTORY

SUMO—Japanese Wrestling, Tourist Library 34 (c.1940) states that Mr. Sigetake Sugiura, who was Emperor Hirohito's tutor, made the following reference to sumo during a lecture on morals to His Imperial Highness:

> *Of all sports in Japan, sumo is the most unique, the like of which is not found anywhere [else] in the world. It is for this reason that the sport is called a national sport…. The practice of Kendo and Zyudo (Judo or Jujitsu) is more or less limited to certain sections of the public, but sumo is practiced by all classes throughout the country, in every town, village, and hamlet, as a medium of physical training and development.*
>
> *One may practice sumo in the hope of becoming an expert, but the fundamental object is the training of mind and heart, the cultivation of a vigorous spirit, and the development of the body. Persons who have learned the art of sumo correctly are, therefore, strongly animated with the spirit of fidelity and sincerity and are courteous and just. They are men of courage who are obedient to reason, and cautious, considerate, and reflective in their mode of living.*
>
> *The controlling, guiding, and unifying spirit in the art of Japanese wrestling is known as Sumodo, or the "Way of the Wrestler."*

The literal translation of sumo is "to mutually rush at" [Su (相)—mutual and Mo (撲)—to rush at].

Sumo wrestling can trace its origins back to ancient time and has long been Japan's national sport. It is performed and watched throughout the country. But sumo is more than just a sport—it is an important part of traditional Japanese culture. Two rivals collide together in the center of the dohyo. The loser is the first to exit the ring or contact the dohyo (ring) floor with any part of his body other than the soles of his feet. Sumo requires no equipment other than a mawashi, but in its simplicity hides a great complexity that encompasses strategy, technique, and psychology. Each bout may be over in an instant, and it isn't always the biggest wrestler who wins.

Sumo was first practiced by the warrior class in Japan. When hand-to-hand combat was more prevalent, the art of wrestling was a valuable skill. During the Shogunate and the Edo period, several Daimyo (feudal lords) began sponsoring the strongest wrestlers, who got big paychecks and Samurai status. Judo was derived from ancient sumo throwing techniques.

As the use of guns and cannons became more common, direct, close range combat became seemingly less important. The sumo rikishi, as sumo wrestlers are known in Japan, were out of a job. These ronin (masterless Samurai) had to make a living somehow and this is when sumo started as a more common form of entertainment and grew into the sport it is today.

Religious organizations began to host sumo tournaments to collect donations for repair of shrines, temples, bridges, and other structures, and also as a way for rikishi to make a living. The rikishi who participated in these tournaments were the first professionals in sumo. During this period, a ranking system was initiated. This also gave birth to the Heya system. A heya is a "team" or "house" that trains rikishi.

At some point, as most civilizations go, a form of women's sumo was being introduced as entertainment for men. As one can imagine this became very risqué. Eventually, as sumo became more popular and widespread, standardized rules were established throughout the country. In order to legitimize sumo into the national sport, women were banned from competing in sumo and actually were forbidden to step onto the dohyo.

Today, professional sumo is Japan's national sport. There are six tournaments (basho) held each year. The tournaments last for fifteen days and each sumotori or rikishi will wrestle seven times for the lower divisions and every day for Juryo and above. The wrestler with the best record at the end wins the tournament. Those who have a winning record (at least 4–3 or 8–7, known as kachi-koshi) will hold their current rank or be promoted. Those who have a losing record (3–4 or 7–8, known as make-koshi) will, more than likely, drop a few ranks.

There are four Americans from Hawaii who did very well in Japan. Each of them had a special impact on Japanese professional sumo.

> **Takamiyama—Jesse Kuhaulua**
>
>   1st foreigner: win championship—July 1972
>
>   take charge of stable (manage team)—Azumazeki
>
>   Highest Rank: Sekiwake—6'4", 450 lbs
>
>   Retired in May, 1984 after twenty years
>
>   Records: Most consecutive tournaments—97 (16+ years)
>
>   Most consecutive bouts—1425
>
> **Konishiki—Saleva'a Atisano'e**
>
>   Highest Rank: Ozeki—6'1", heaviest rikishi (626 lbs)
>
>   Retired in November, 1997—won 3 tournaments
>
> **Akebono—Chad Rowan**
>
>   Highest Rank: 1st foreign Yokozuna (64th)—6'8", 520 lbs
>
>   Retired in January, 2001—won 11 tournaments

Musashimaru—Fiamalu Penitani
Highest Rank: Yokozuna (67th)—6'3", 520 lbs
Retired in November. 2003—won 12 tournaments

Sumo is also an amateur sport in Japan, with participants in colleges, high schools, and grade schools throughout the country. To encourage the sport's development worldwide, the governing body for sumo in Japan, the Nihon Sumo Kyokai, established the International Sumo Federation (IFS) to preside over amateur sumo globally.

Due to Japan's effort to create world-wide interest in sumo, it is increasing its international profile. Sumo has national clubs in over 85 countries and an IFS member country hosts an international World Sumo Championship each year.

In 1980, the first All-Japan Amateur Sumo Championships were held. Teams from overseas were invited to compete, and this became the first international amateur sumo tournament held anywhere in the world.

The ultimate goal of the IFS is to make sumo a truly international sport and to get sumo into the Olympics. Although sumo has not yet achieved its dream of becoming an Olympic sport, it is part of major multi-sport international competitions: sumo is in the quadrennial World Games and is also one of the 13 martial arts in the biennial World Combat Games. With the goal of getting sumo into the Olympics in mind, the IFS made a few adjustments to the established rules in sumo.

The biggest change was to allow women to compete. The International Olympic Committee established that any new sport admitted into the Olympics had to be open to both men and women. In 1997, the first major sumo championship for women was held in Japan. Shin Sumo—or "new sumo"—had 80 registered women in Japan in 1996, over 800 registered in 2007, and now has over 40 countries that participate in the Women World Sumo Championships each year.

Another concession was to institute weight classes. The professional ranks in Japan do not have weight classes, but amateur sumo has four (4) divisions for both men and women (light-, middle-, heavy-, and open-weight), along with various classifications for juniors.

A third compromise of the IFS, because of religious and cultural differences in various countries, is that athletes are allowed to wear shorts under the mawashi. This makes sumo more family-friendly. Women wear a one-piece body suit or leotard under the mawashi.

Amateur sumo is particularly strong throughout Europe. Some Eastern European athletes have been successful enough to be scouted into professional sumo in Japan.

The U.S. Sumo Federation (USSF) is the governing body in the United States. Amateur sumo clubs are gaining in popularity and competitions are regularly being hosted across the country. The sport has always been popular on the West Coast and in Hawaii, where it has been part of the local Japanese community festivals.

Amateur sumo has grown in the U.S., and athletes come from a variety of ethnic, cultural, and sporting backgrounds. Many athletes come to the sport from a background in judo, freestyle wrestling, other grappling sports, bodybuilding, football, and mixed martial arts.

A USSF goal is to raise the proficiency level of our athletes so that Americans can participate more competitively on the world stage. We also love to share our knowledge and skill of the sport with others who are interested in learning the rich cultural history of Japan and sumo.

The following Americans have done well in the amateur world of sumo by medaling at the World Sumo Championship level:

Name	Year	Category	Medal
Emanuel Yarbrough	1992	Open-weight	Silver
	1993	Open-weight	Bronze
	1994	Open-weight	Silver
	1995	Open-weight	GOLD
	1996	Open-weight	Silver
Hideo Su'a	1992	Heavy-weight	Silver
Nobuo Tsuchiya	1994	Light-weight	Bronze
Wayne Vierra	1997	Heavy-weight	Bronze
Harrington Wa'a	1999	Junior Open-weight	GOLD
Gregory Donofrio	2001	Junior Middle-weight	Bronze
Trent Sabo	2008	Light-weight	Bronze

Sumo is a contact sport and can be very rough. That roughness keeps some people away and attracts others. An average match lasts just a matter of seconds. It's amazingly explosive. The burst of energy and adrenaline makes sumo as physically and mentally intense as any sport can be.

Sumo is not for everyone, but those who give it a try and stick with it are not disappointed in the spirit, passion, and camaraderie of the athletes they meet and compete against.

TYPICAL SUMO WORKOUT REGIMEN

Shinkyaku (leg stretch) — 8–12 each

    4 times to each side – 8 count

Shiko (leg lifts) — 50–100 each

    Koshiwari Squat – 8 count – with hands resting on knees

    Koshiwari Squat – 8 count – with elbows inside as in chugoshi

Suriashi (basic movement – sliding feet)

Masugu (straight)	5–10 each
Migi (right)	5–10 each
Hidari (left)	5–10 each
Hop / squat (straight)	5–10 each with 8-count squat on last one

Spar — 5–10 each

    King of the Dohyo - winner stays

    While waiting – weights, tsuparri pole, shiko, suriashi

Butsukari (Oshi/Push drill)

    5–10 each individual with 8-count squat at end

Shiko — 30–50 each

    Koshiwari Squat – 8 count – with hands resting on knees

    Koshiwari Squat – 8 count – with elbows inside as in chugoshi

Sonkyo Meditation

    Eyes closed, breathe deeply, relax

Sensei Greeting

    Bow and shake hands with sensei

WEIGHT DIVISIONS

In Japan, professional sumo does not have any weight classes. A professional sumo rikishi must meet a certain height requirement but there is no weight requirement or divisions. An average professional wrestler weighs in at about 160 kg or 353 lbs. There are some who are smaller than that and there are some who are much heavier. The largest rikishi weighed in at over 700 lbs.

Divisions in the professional ranks are based on performance. If, at the end of the tournament, you have a win/loss record greater than .500, you will probably move up in rank. If your win/loss record is below .500, you most likely move down in rank. Your rank will determine what division you are placed in.

Normally, when amateur athletes compete in Japan at local, prefectural, or even national levels, they do not use weight classes. Amateur divisions in Japan are divided by age. Only when competing on an international level do the Japanese athletes split into weight divisions.

Amateur sumo, which is governed by the IFS on an international level, has established weight classes or divisions. Currently, the IFS recognizes three (3) weight classes in both the men and women senior divisions along with an "open" division that may pit rikishi in different weight categories against each other. IFS sanctioned events, such as the World Sumo Championships, World Games, and World Combat Games, use these four divisions for athletes to compete in. The divisions and their respective weights are as follows:

Men—IFS		
Division	kg	lbs
Light	85	187
Middle	115	253
Heavy	115+	253+

Women—IFS		
Division	kg	lbs
Light	65	143
Middle	80	176
Heavy	80+	176+

Junior Men (13–18)—IFS		
Division	kg	lbs
Light	80	176
Middle	100	220
Heavy	100+	220+

Junior Women (13–18)—IFS		
Division	kg	lbs
Light	60	132
Middle	75	165
Heavy	75+	165+

In some European circles, there have been additional weight classes. In the divisions established by the IFS, as you see above, each men's class is divided into weights of 30+ kilograms or 60+ pounds. In the European model below, the categories are only half that amount.

Men's Divisions		kg	lbs
Div I	Feather	70	154
Div II	Light	85	187
Div III	Welter	100	220
Div IV	Middle	115	253
Div V	Cruiser	130	286
Div VI	Heavy	130+	286+

Women's Divisions		kg	lbs
Div I	Feather	55	121
Div II	Light	65	143
Div III	Welter	75	165
Div IV	Middle	85	187
Div V	Cruiser	95	209
Div VI	Heavy	95+	209+

Because of the increased number of divisions: a) more individuals have an opportunity to win a medal, and b) more importantly, athletes are wrestling against someone more comparable in size.

In the IFS system, a rikishi that is at the bottom end of his weight class is giving up almost 30 kilos or 60 pounds to his opponent if his opponent is at the other end of the division. In the European model, an athlete is only giving 15 kilos or 30 pounds to his opponent.

Many athletes do not want to give that much of a weight advantage (60 pounds) to their opponent and would like to see additional weight classes added.

Another "open" division could also be added: a "Light Open" and a "Heavy Open." The "Light Open" would include the feather-, light-, and welter-weight classes and the "Heavy Open" would include the middle-, cruiser-, and heavy-weight divisions.

> NOTE: In the United States, we have a small children's (under age 13) division and junior (age 13–18) competitions at the national, state, and local levels along with a Masters (starting at age 40) division.

Chapter 2

THE MAWASHI

The only uniform item of a sumotori is called a mawashi, or loincloth. Some people outside the sumo world may refer to the mawashi as a diaper—you just have to grin and bear (bare) it. Most dedicated sumotori have a sense of humor and knowing the purpose and function of the mawashi, such comments don't bother them. A professional's mawashi in Japan is made of silk, while practice and most amateur's mawashi are made of a thick canvas material.

SIZE

Length varies depending on the girth of the rikishi, normally 24–28 feet or approximately 7–9 meters long. It is 18 inches or 47 centimeters wide.

> Note: Japan is the best source to obtain an authentic mawashi as far as thickness and width. There are Internet sites to obtain these from Japan. As a substitute, sumotori in the U.S. can have one made at most any canvas company. The #4 (25.54 oz thick) canvas, 18" wide, is very close in thickness to a Japanese mawashi. The lighter, more pliable, #6 (21.27 oz) canvas is a good alternative for a child's mawashi.

WEAR OF GARMENTS

For cultural, modesty, and religious reasons, and the fact that club mawashi may be used by various members, the IFS has approved the use of shorts under the mawashi for men and boys. The pants should be black, made of tight fitting material (e.g., cycling pants), and come to mid-thigh.

Women should wear a leotard or other tight fitting clothing of any color under the mawashi. This can be mid-thigh or longer on the leg.

> Note: The Japanese call the shorts "spats" and translate it as "underpants" in their rules. This may lead people to think that wearing underpants is acceptable. It is not.

Loose clothing presents two dangers:

1) exposure of what should be hidden, and

2) being grasped or pulled by your opponent on purpose or accidentally while trying to execute a grip.

The latter is prohibited and if anything other than the mawashi (e.g., clothes, bandages, or supporters) is grasped twice or more, it will result in a loss for the one who grabs it.

The mawashi must be tied tightly. A loss of the mawashi or if the front part of the mawashi comes undone during a match, for male or female, the wearer will be declared to have lost the match.

HOW TO FOLD

Fold in half lengthwise twice (¼).

> Note: The interior of the first fold should be approximately ¼–½ inch shorter than the exterior so that when the second fold is made it will not overlap the outside of the exterior of the mawashi.

The mawashi should be 4 ½–4 ¾ inches wide after it is folded in half twice.

> Note: The best way to get a nice flat fold is to take an 8" long piece of two-by-four and run it along the crease of the fold as you fold it down the length of the mawashi. The best way to soften it is by running it through the washer a few times with fabric softener. You can throw it in the dryer, too; it actually dries pretty fast.

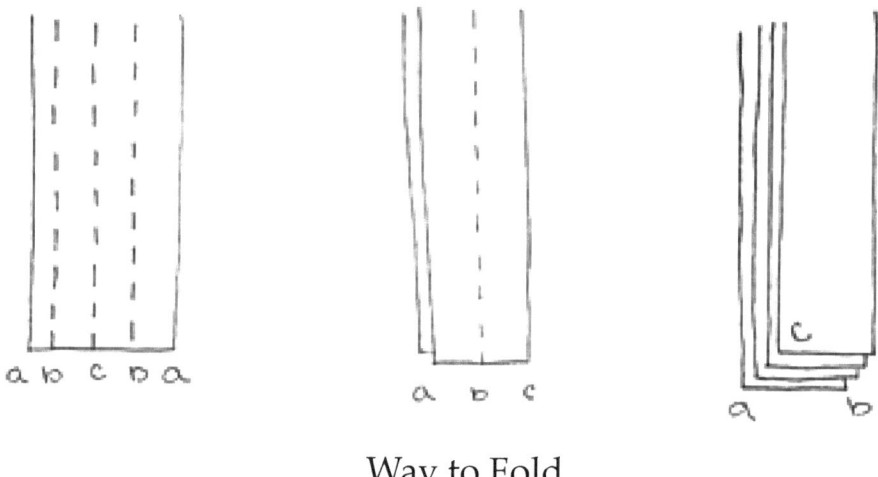

Way to Fold

HOW TO TIE

Step 1: From approximately 36 to 60 inches from one end, fold in half again (⅛).

This will be the part that fits between your legs and covers the buttocks.

Step 2: Place triple-folded area between your legs while a helper holds the mawashi behind you.

The open-ended and creased side is placed on top or on the inside.

The creased side is placed downward or outside.

Step 3: Unfold the first 36 inches (½) of the mawashi to form a pocket to hold your privates.

Adjust the portion around the crotch area to get a good fit.

The end of the mawashi should be about neck high.

Step 4: After forming the pocket, hold the front of the mawashi with your right hand about chest high.

Step 5: Reach around with your left hand to hold the mawashi with your palm facing outward on the small of your back (Figure A).

Figure A   Figure B   Figure C

Step 6: While holding the front and back, begin to turn clockwise (right) while your helper holds the mawashi (Figure B).

Release the mawashi as it tightens around your back side (Figure C).

Stop when the mawashi reaches the left side after the second wrap in front.

Step 7: Adjust and tighten the mawashi around the waist and crotch areas.

Step 8: Let the beginning of the mawashi drop in front of the second wrap (Figure D).

It will be covered with the next wrap around (Figure E).

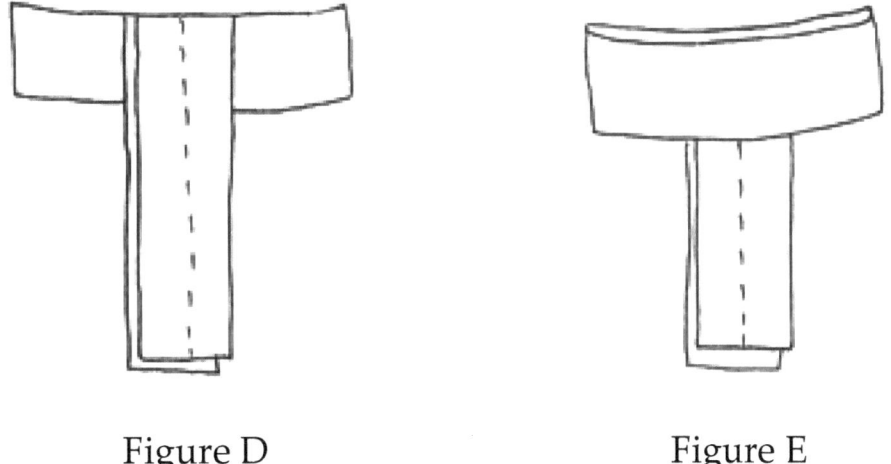

Figure D   Figure E

Step 9: Resume turning clockwise until you reach the left side again.

Adjust and tighten the crotch area if necessary.

Step 10: Fold the beginning of the mawashi in half and at an angle, up and to the right, on the next wrap (Figure F and G).

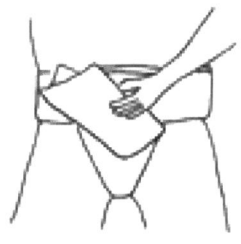

Figure F   Figure G

Step 11: Resume clockwise turning.

Adjust and tighten if necessary.

The mawashi should end close to your navel in order to have enough to tie in the back.

Step 12: Your helper should fold the last 27–30 inches of the mawashi in half again (⅛).

Step 13: Your helper will slip the folded portion under all the wraps (to include the very first portion from between your legs) and up through the small of your back (Figure H).

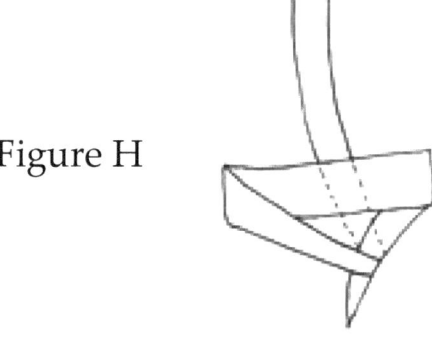

Figure H

To tighten, lay the end over forearm and pull up and/or have the wearer squat.

Step 14: Take the end and bring it down and through the very last wrap (Figures I and J). Pull tight.

Figure I   Figure J

Now you are ready to sumo!

Sumo Skills: Instructional Guide for Competitive Sumo

Front View

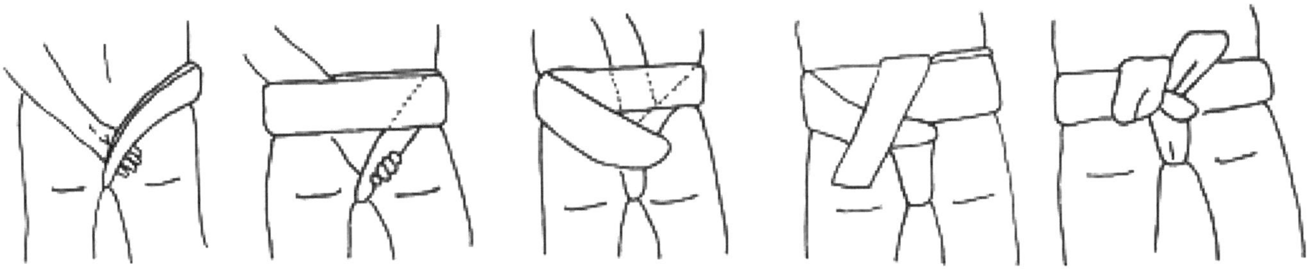

Back View

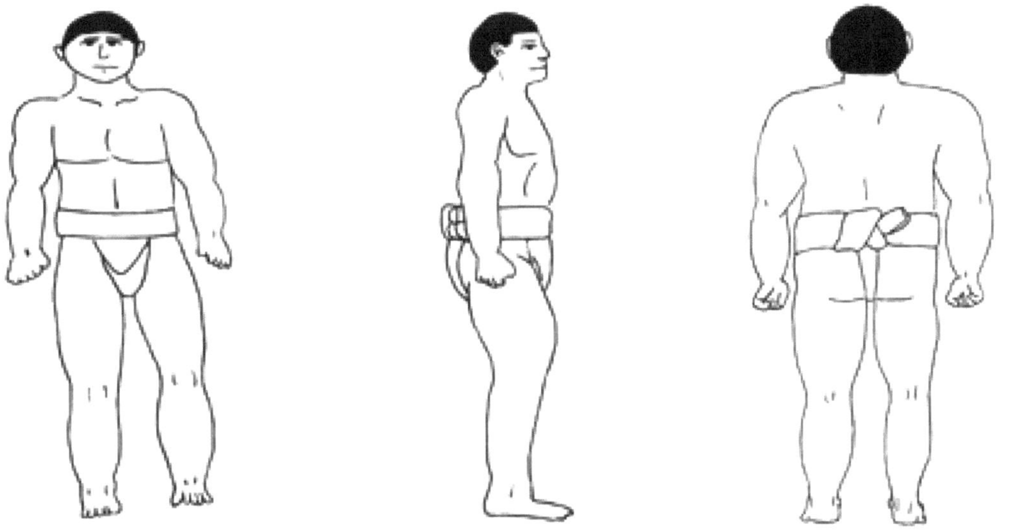

Full View

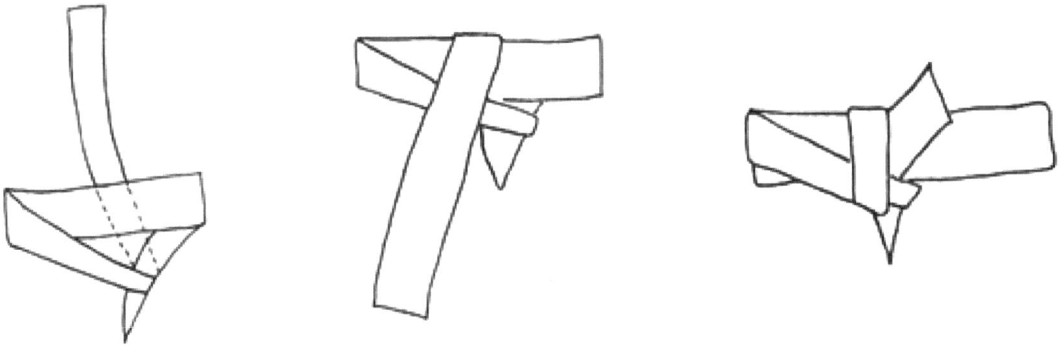

How to Tie

13

Chapter 3

THE REFEREE (GYOJI) AND JUDGES (SHINPAN)

Whenever possible, a sumo competition's judges comprise six judges chosen from a pool of recognized judges:

    1 each   Chief Judge (Shinpan Cho)
    1 each   Referee (Gyoji)
    4 each   Ringside Judges (Shinpan)

Note: Smaller competitions use at a minimum a gyoji and at least one other judge.

The decision of a match is made by these six judges. Their decision is final.

POSITIONING OF JUDGES

The judges should enter and exit the dohyo-damari (ringside waiting area) as a group.

While standing in front of their seats, the judges make a bow at the command of the gyoji.

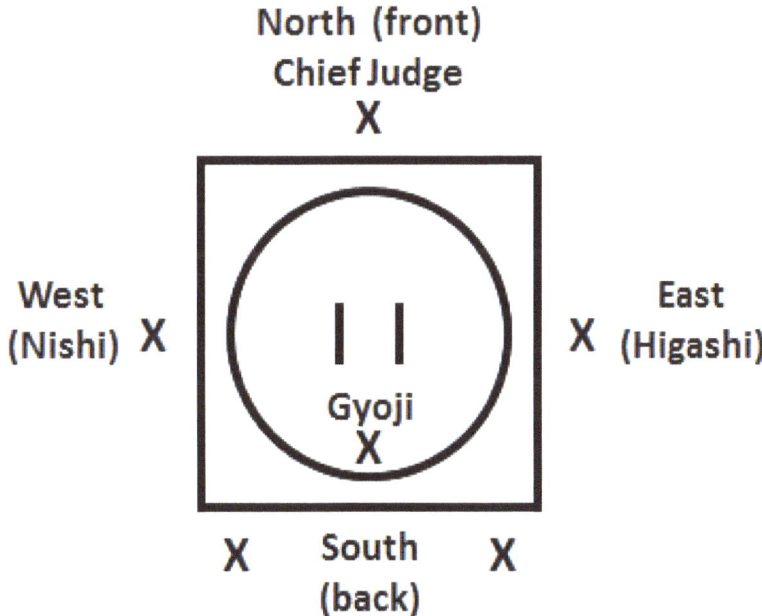

Ringside Judges

The referee, or gyoji, oversees the action in the dohyo, signals the start of the bouts, keeps the action going, watches for unauthorized techniques, and declares the winner.

The gyoji enters and exits with the other judges and is positioned in front of their seats.

The gyoji gives a command, "bow" ("Rei!"); all the judges (shinpan) bow and then are seated.

The gyoji's position is the south or back side, outside the outer area of the dohyo.

PRELIMINARY ACTIONS

The gyoji must carry out his actions in the dohyo in a swift and orderly manner, taking care not to impede the movements of the rikishi.

The gyoji and rikishi enter the dohyo at their respective tawara (toku-dawara, or corner). The gyoji steps into the ring while the rikishi should position themselves just outside the toku-dawara, waiting for a signal from the gyoji to enter. The gyoji may signal the rikishi to enter the dohyo with his hands or a nod of the head. The rikishi step into the dohyo. The gyoji will then give the command of "bow" ("Rei!"). The rikishi bow to each other.

The gyoji waits just inside the toku-dawara, feet together at the heels with toes pointed at a 45-degree angle, hands straight along the side of his body while the rikishi perform the ritual of showing their opponent that they are not concealing any weapons (chirichozu). (See Figure 1.)

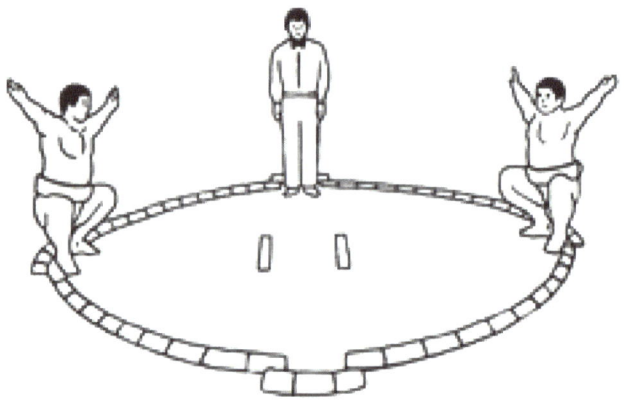

Figure 1

As the rikishi step forward to squat (sonkyo), the gyoji also takes two steps forward, standing in front of and between the starting lines (shikirisen). (See Figure 2.) When the rikishi are balanced and are relaxed during sonkyo, the gyoji will shout, "Get ready" ("Kamaete!").

Figure 2

STARTING THE MATCH

When the rikishi stand and step back, the gyoji takes one and a half steps backward with both legs spread at a 45-degree angle, knees slightly bent, with both arms extended with palms facing inward. (See Figures 3 and 4.)

The gyoji shouts, "Get ready with your hands" ("Te o tsuite, mattanashi!") to signal the rikishi to get in the set position of shikiri.

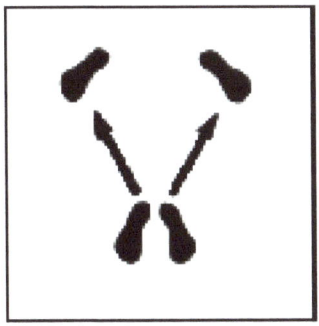

Figure 3

Figure 4

If one rikishi is in the set position with both hands on the surface of the dohyo before the other rikishi has both hands touching the dohyo, the gyoji may say, "not yet, not yet" ("Mada yo, mada yo!") and indicate to the second rikishi to place both hands on the dohyo by saying, "Te o tsuite, te o tsuite!"

After both rikishi touch the surface of the dohyo with both hands, the gyoji gives the signal to start by shouting "Go" ("Hakke-yoi!") to the rikishi, who start the tachiai. (See Figures 4 and 5.)

Figure 5

RULES OF THE TACHIAI

The tachiai is started by the shout "Hakke-yoi!" of the gyoji.

The rikishi's hands must touch down behind the starting lines (shikirisen).

> Note: It is not recognized at the tachiai in amateur sumo to touch the surface of the dohyo momentarily or make a motion to touch as the professionals do in Japan. Amateur rikishi must wait on the gyoji to start the match.

If a rikishi begins the tachiai before the gyoji shouts "Hakke-yoi!" the gyoji must shout "wait" ("Matta!") and start the tachiai again.

THE MATCH

During the bout, the gyoji must always try to be in the best position to easily observe the outcome of a match and maintain a posture suitable for delivery of a verdict.

The gyoji must take care not to step on the straw bags forming the perimeter of the dohyo (shodu-dawara) or on the fine sand just outside the dohyo (janome). (This is not as critical for an inside, portable dohyo).

During the match, a gyoji may encourage the rikishi. These phrases are called kakegoe.

"Nokatta, nokatta!"—said at the tachiai and when a rikishi is executing a technique.

"Yoi, hakke-yoi!"—encouraging rikishi to try harder and to get out of an immobile state.

TEMPORARY HALT OR RESTART OF A MATCH

When a mawashi comes loose, the gyoji may halt the bout by shouting, "Matta!" (wait) and putting a hand on each rikishi to signal them to stop. This is called a "mawashi matta."

Both rikishi should remain in the exact position of when the gyoji touches them. The gyoji will tighten the mawashi and restart the match. The match is restarted by the gyoji placing a hand on each rikishi. When the gyoji lifts his hands and shouts "Hakke-yoi!" the rikishi may begin again.

If the rikishi move out of position and cannot satisfactorily be repositioned, the shinpan cho (head judge) may order the match to be restarted.

DECISION OF THE GYOJI

The gyoji makes the initial decision of who won, upon completion of a match.

There are only two (2) ways to win a match in sumo:

1. To force your opponent to touch the surface of the dohyo with any part of the body other than the bottoms of the feet, and

2. To force your opponent to touch anywhere outside the dohyo with any part of the body before you do.

There are two (2) exceptions to the two ways to win a match printed above:

1. A rikishi is performing tsuridashi (lift out, or similar technique). He is allowed to place one foot out of the dohyo and place his opponent on the ground. The rikishi must have full control of his opponent before he steps out. This is done for safety to prevent injury to either rikishi. The match is over when the rikishi steps out and before his opponent is placed on the ground.

2. Both rikishi are falling and one rikishi is directly impacting on top of the other. The rikishi on top may put his hand down before his opponent touches to break his fall so that he does not crush his opponent, who is underneath him.

Note: This is rarely used in a decision but is a possibility if the rikishi are falling in an awkward position when an injury will occur to one of them and/or the top rikishi was in full control at the time of falling. This is performed by one of the rikishi for safety and recognized by the gyoji and/or judges.

There are also seven (7) ways to be disqualified during a sumo match:

1. If the vertical part of the front of the mawashi (maebukuro) gets loose and out of place,
2. When a rikishi uses a prohibited technique (see Prohibited Techniques),
3. When a competitor is ruled unable to continue because of an injury,
4. If the competitor arbitrarily terminates the bout,
5. If the rikishi does not follow the judge's instructions,
6. If it is ruled that a rikishi deliberately failed to jump off to begin the bout,
7. When the athlete fails to appear in the dohyo-damari (ringside waiting area) after being called twice by the broadcasting staff.

At the end of a match, the gyoji immediately shouts, "the contest is over" ("Shobu atta!") and indicates with his arm the East or the West winning rikishi (depending on the side from which they entered). (See Figure 6.)

Figure 6

When the match is over, the rikishi and the gyoji return to their starting positions just inside the toku-dawara. The gyoji says, "bow" ("Rei!"), to which the rikishi respond to by bowing to each other. (See Figure 7.)

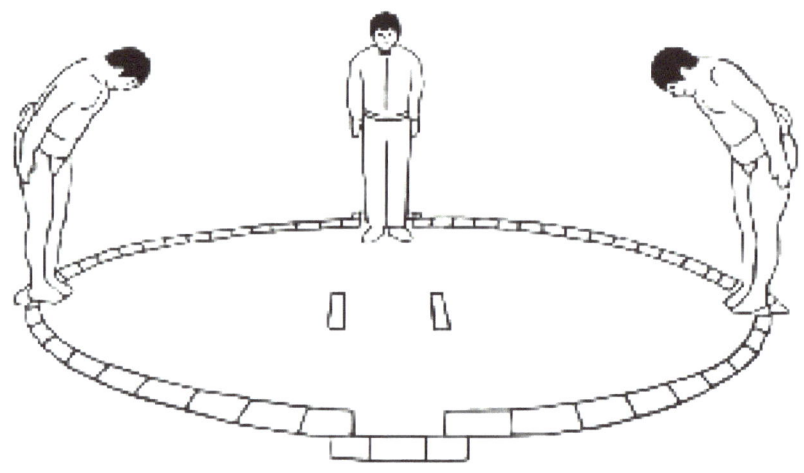

Figure 7

If there are no objections by the shinpan, the gyoji then makes a formal declaration of the winner by saying, "the West (East) is the winner" ("Nishi (Higashi) no kachi!") and signaling with his arm in the direction of the winning rikishi. (See Figure 8.)

> Note: Higashi (East) is always to the gyoji's right; Nishi (West) is always to the gyoji's left.

Figure 8

The loser takes a step back and down from the dohyo. The winning rikishi assumes the sonkyo position to receive the decision.

> Note: In the case of team contests, before the first bout and after the last bout, the contestants from each team must line up on the East and West sides of the dohyo respectively and the gyoji, standing inside the toku-dawara, will instruct them by saying, "bow" ("Rei!").

CHALLENGES BY THE SHINPAN:

The judges monitor the tachiai carefully and stop the match if either rikishi does not start properly.

In addition, any one of the judges may challenge a decision made by the gyoji. If there is a disagreement, the shinpan must immediately raise his right hand before the gyoji has given the kachi-nanori (formal announcement). Once the gyoji makes the final announcement, the decision is final and no objections may be raised.

The rikishi will exit the dohyo and wait for the shinpan committee to determine a winner.

The shinpan meet in the center of the dohyo to discuss the verdict in a conference (mono-ii). (See Figure 9.)

Figure 9

The chief judge (shinpan cho) presides over the mono-ii.

The judge who raised his hand should state the reason he challenges the initial decision of the gyoji.

The gyoji should then explain what he saw and the reason for his decision.

The next step is for all the judges to talk and make a ruling.

The final decision is based on a majority vote and is announced by the chief judge.

Upon returning to their seats, the chief judge can concur with the gyoji's verdict (gunbai dori), declare a complete reversal of the decision (sashichigai), or call for a rematch (tori-naoshi).

If the judging committee agrees with the initial decision, the initial winning rikishi steps into the dohyo and performs sonkyo to accept the decision.

If the committee rules opposite of the gyoji's decision, the winning rikishi steps into the dohyo and performs sonkyo to accept the decision.

If a decision cannot be made, the match will be replayed (tori-naoshi). Both rikishi step into the dohyo and start the pre-match ritual.

DIALOGUE OF THE GYOJI

Signal the rikishi to enter the ring, bow, and complete ring entering:

    Rei (Bow)

After ring entering:

    Kamaete (Get ready)

After sonkyo (rest stance) to signal the rikishi to get in the set position of shikiri for tachiai:

    Te o tsuite, mattanashi (Get your hands ready, no waiting)

Signal tachiai:

    Hakke-yoi (Go)

    Nokatta, nokatta—said at the tachiai and when a rikishi is executing a technique

    Yoi, hakke-yoi—encouraging the rikishi to try harder and to get out of an immobile state

While indicating with your arm the winning rikishi:

    Shobu atta (The contest is over)

After the rikishi return to their respective side:

    Rei (Bow)

While indicating with your arm the winning rikishi:

    Higashi no kachi (The East is the winner) (right)

    Nishi no kachi (The West is the winner) (left)

Chapter 4
FUNDAMENTAL SUMO MOVEMENTS

There are several basic positions and movements in sumo.

Sonkyo (squatting), chirchozu (greeting), chugoshi (proper posture), and shikiri (set position) are posture positions. Movements include shiko, koshiwari, shinyaku, matawari, teppo, suriashi, and ukemi, which serve as methods of training.

Three of these are especially key and are essential to a successful rikishi: chugoshi, shiko, and suriashi. These movements not only build muscle and maintain one's center and balance, but also position the body low and anchored to the dohyo.

These are symbolic movements and are the foundation of sumo. Rikishi must understand and grasp the meaning of these movements and strive to perform these movements well.

SONKYO

Sonkyo (squatting) is a form of greeting or salute. A rikishi takes this position at the beginning and end of a match, giving his salute to his opponent. You must always start and end a sumo match by paying respect to your opponent, whether you are the winner or loser.

HOW TO PERFORM SONKYO

FIGURE 1

Squat with knees apart; keep balance by stretching knees apart as far as they can go.

Thrust out chest, throw back and relax the shoulders.

Create your center of gravity in the lower abdomen.

Place hands on each knee in a soft fist

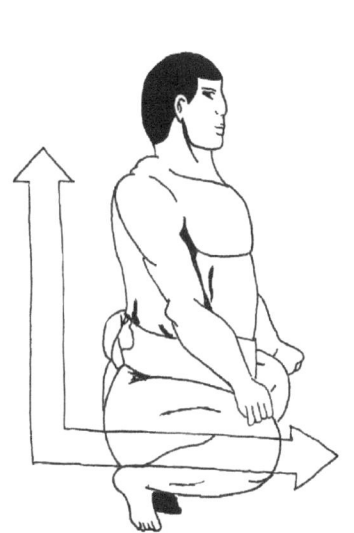

FIGURE 2

Drop and pull in jaw naturally.

Look straight ahead.

Drop hips deep; buttocks should rest on heels.

Back should remain upright and straight.

Do not lean forward with upper body.

CHIRICHOZU

Chirichozu is another salute of sumo, performed after stepping into the dohyo and taking a bow when preparing for a match. Both rikishi perform this movement at the same time to show each other respect, to demonstrate that they will fight a fair match and they do not possess any weapons, and also to prepare mentally for the upcoming match. This is the dohyo-iri or ring entering ceremony.

HOW TO PERFORM CHIRICHOZU

Step 1

After the gyoji (referee) signals, step inside the dohyo tawara and bow to your opponent.

Start by taking the position of sonkyo, placing your hands on each knee.

Step 2

Place hands on the outside of knees with palms facing downward.

Salute (bow) by bending upper body forward (approx. 15-degree angle).

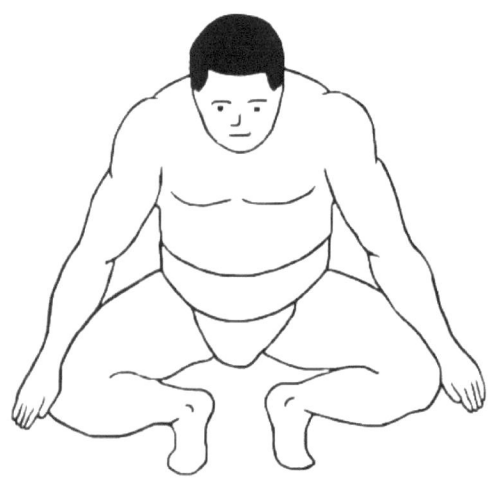

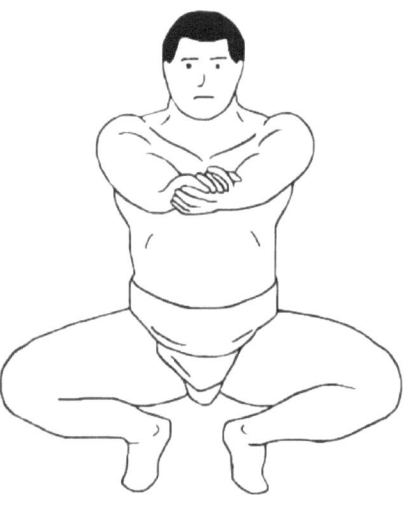

Step 3

Position both hands in front of the chest.

Begin with the right palm over the left; turn hands over so that the left palm is over the right.

This signifies the washing of your hands, cleansing yourself before the match.

Sumo Skills: Instructional Guide for Competitive Sumo

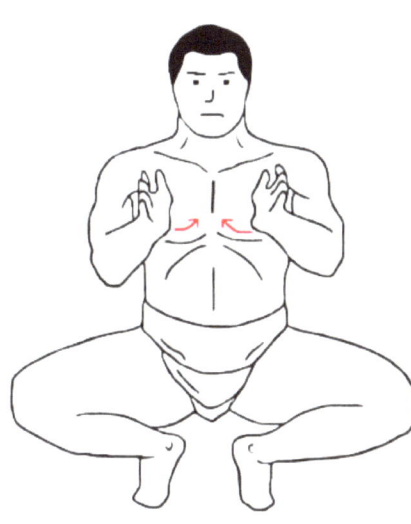

Step 4

With palms facing out, raise hands about head high.

Make a circle with palms facing each other.

Clap once as the hands come together.

This signifies the athletes getting the attention of the spirits.

Step 5

Hold hands together momentarily, palms facing each other.

Step 6

Open palms, without separating the pinky fingers of both hands, similar to opening a book.

This signifies opening a religious book—praying for strength, good sportsmanship, and no injuries.

Step 7

Raise arms to the side turning the palms upward.

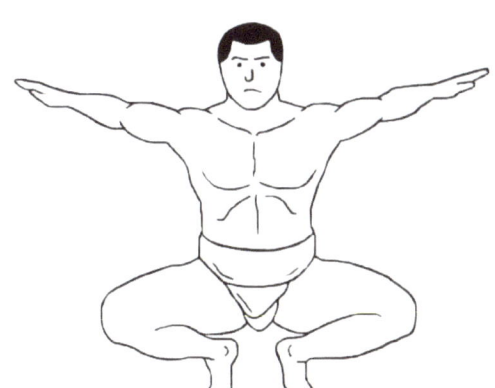

Step 8

Turn both palms downward.

Both of these moves signify showing your opponent that you come to the match with no weapons.

POSTURE OF CHUGOSHI

Chugoshi is the most ideal position to be in during a sumo match.

A rikishi, when in proper chugoshi posture, can move quickly and be in control of the match. It is important to train in this position to not only keep your balance and center of gravity, but also so it becomes second nature while you are in a match.

HOW TO PERFORM CHUGOSHI

Spread legs a little wider than the shoulders.

Lock elbows to sides.

Forearms extended forward, hands slightly cupped with palms facing inward.

Arch the back a little.

Pull jaw into neck, keep eyes on opponent.

ANGLES OF CHUGOSHI

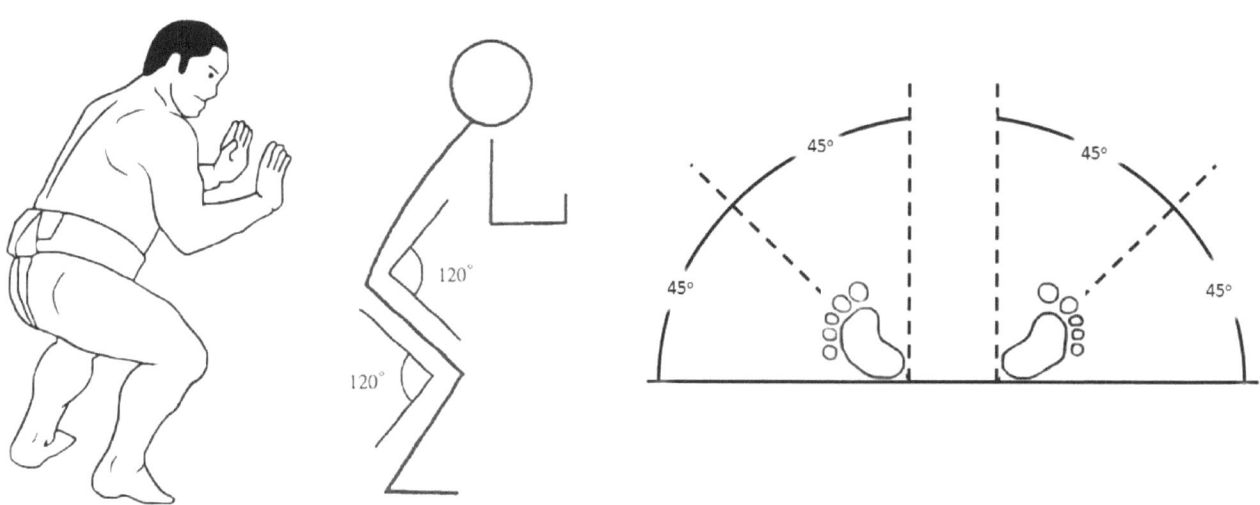

SHINKYAKU

The shinkyaku stretch enhances the flexibility of the legs and strengthens the hips. It is also a warm up for the more advanced matawari stretch.

HOW TO PERFORM SHINKYAKU

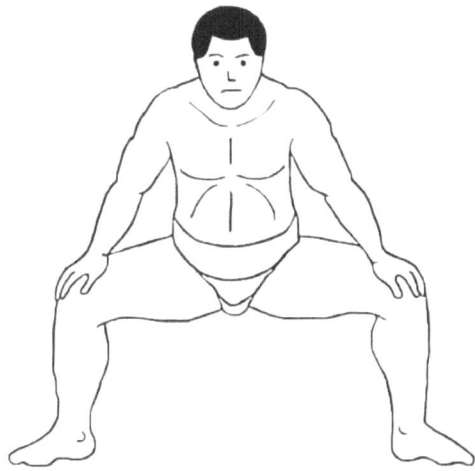

Step 1

Open the stance of shiko a bit wider.

Pull your hips forward.

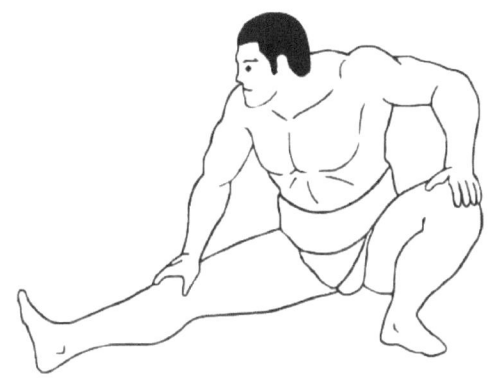

Step 2

Place palms on each knee.

Straighten right leg firmly by shifting weight onto heel of lead (left) leg without leaning forward.

Do not raise the heel of the lead leg off the dohyo.

Step 3

Point the toes of the outstretched leg inward.

Drop the thigh down deeply so that it touches the dohyo.

Repeat this movement with right and left leg alternately.

SHIKO

The shiko is the most fundamental, basic, and important training exercise in sumo.

The shiko not only strengthens the lower body but also strengthens the spine. It develops a sense of balance and pliability. In addition, one can master how to shift his weight and still maintain a balanced center of gravity. Watching an individual perform shiko will reveal how skillful and how strong the rikishi is.

HOW TO PERFORM SHIKO

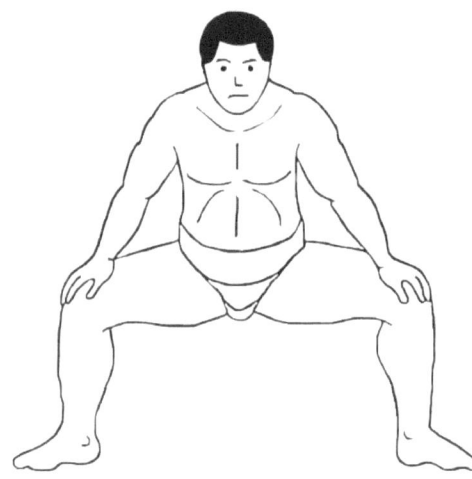

Step 1

Spread legs apart and extend the tips of the toes outward at an angle of 120 degrees.

Drop hips down to a right angle or lower.

Place both hands on the knees softly.

Keep hips forward; remain upright; do not lean forward.

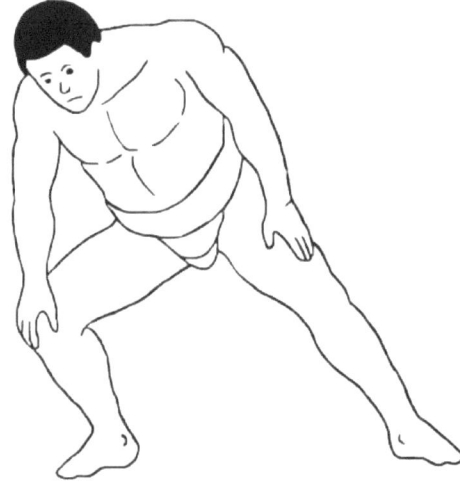

Step 2

Begin by shifting your weight to the lead (left) leg. Always start by raising the right leg.

Keep force on inside of leg and on the big toe.

The lead leg should still be bent, shift the weight.

DO NOT straighten your lead leg or stand up.

Begin to breathe in.

Step 3

While shifting weight onto the lead leg, raise the other (right) leg.

Eyes should be focused on your toes.

Left hand remains on knee to help stabilize and balance; right hand may move slightly above the knee.

Continue to breathe in.

Step 4

Straighten both legs.

Left hand remains on knee to stabilize and balance; right hand remains just above the right knee or may move behind upper thigh.

It is important to raise the leg as high as possible.

Stop your breathing.

Step 5

Hold at highest position for 2–3 seconds.

Lower the raised leg from the tip of the toe first.

Breathe out.

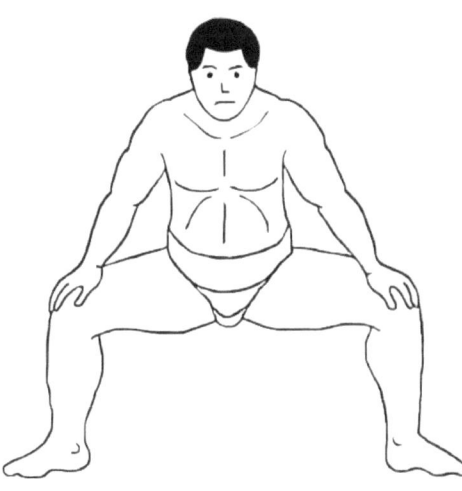

Step 6

Come back to the first position; squat. Hips remain forward—keep shoulders back; do not lean upper body forward.

Lead hand remains on knee; other (right) hand slaps above knee as foot lands on dohyo.

Stop breathing.

Repeat movement alternating right/left legs.

KOSHIWARI

Performing koshiwari will aid in maintaining your sumo posture by giving you flexibility. This exercise will help to lower your hips while maintaining your stability and center of gravity. It conditions the flexibility of the hip joint and the elasticity of the knees.

Koshiwari is an important movement usually incorporated immediately following shiko, performing two eight-count repetitions.

HOW TO PERFORM KOSHIWARI

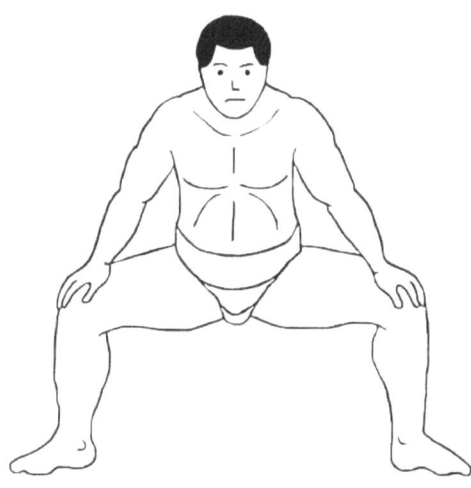

Step 1

Take the position of shiko.

Pull your hips forward.

Step 2

Drop your hips deep; squat as low as you can; place hands on your knee (as in step 1) or on your thighs (as in step 2).

Hold for an eight count—you may bounce a little to get a deeper squat.

It is important to keep your body upright and your hips forward and to face straight ahead.

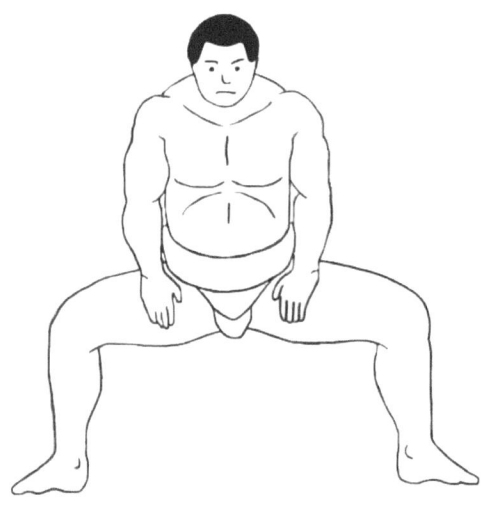

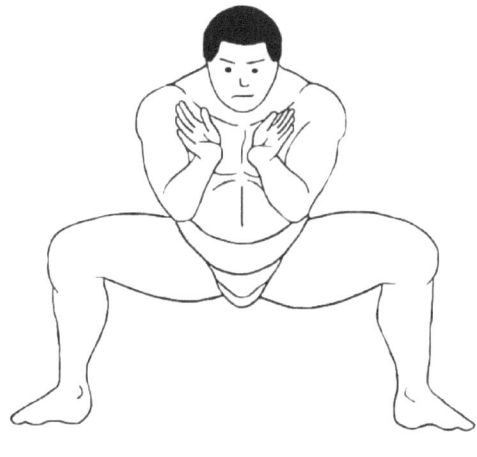

Step 3

Continue to squat as low as you can, keeping your hips forward and your body upright.

Drop you chin down to your chest.

Pin your elbows to your side and raise your hands with palms facing outward.

Hold for another eight-count.

SURIASHI (HAKOBIASHI)

Suriashi is a basic but foundational movement of sumo. It is a movement peculiar to sumo. To advance or move forward during a match, one should always use suriashi.

Suriashi is sliding or shuffling one's foot across the dohyo without separating the pad of the big toe from the dohyo, throwing your weight on the inside of your feet, and keeping a low center of gravity. A rikishi depends on this technique to gain a superior position from shikiri (fighting stance) to tachiai (initial charge). It is used throughout the match and allows the rikishi to always keep his balance.

> Note: Because your big toes should never leave the dohyo, they are considered a "power point." Once a big toe separates from the dohyo, your center of gravity—your power—can be altered rather quickly. The palm area of your pinky finger is also considered another "power point." When a rikishi is applying a technique, whether it is pushing, thrusting, throwing, or pulling, he is normally using his hand(s). The majority of his power generates from the palm area of the pinky finger.

HOW TO PERFORM SURIASHI

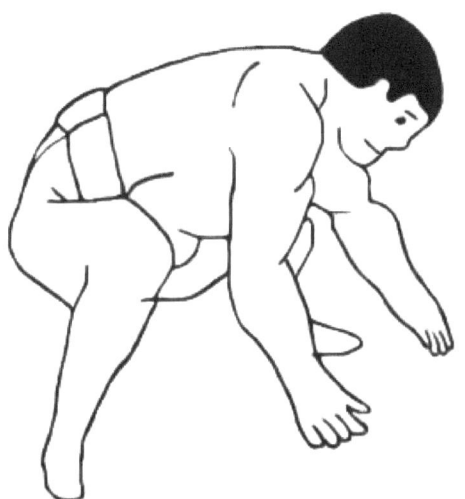

Step 1

Begin in the position of shikiri, the basic fighting stance.

Step 2

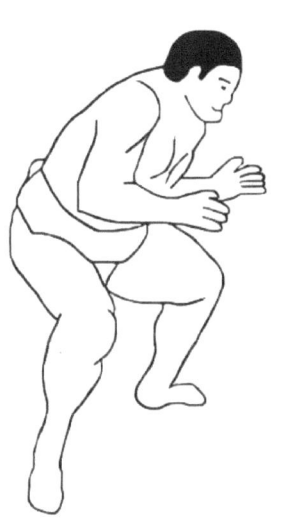

As you start the initial charge, pin elbows to sides with forearms straight out, palms facing inward.

Do not straighten/stand up—your first movement should take you straight ahead, keeping your center of gravity low.

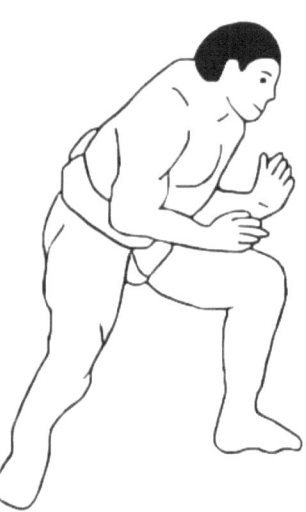

Step 3

Slide or shuffle foot forward.

Keep big toe anchored on dohyo.

Shift weight onto inside of feet.

Step 4

Slide or shuffle other foot forward.

Keep center of gravity low.

Keep elbows pinned to side, forearms out, palms facing inward.

Do not waddle side to side; movement is straight forward.

Step 5

Advance to the edge of the dohyo—squat deeply.

Stretch arms forward as you come out of squat position. Do not step while stretching your arms forward; you want to remain inside the dohyo.

FIGURE 1 Pattern on the dohyo

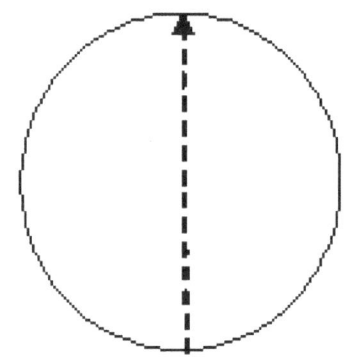

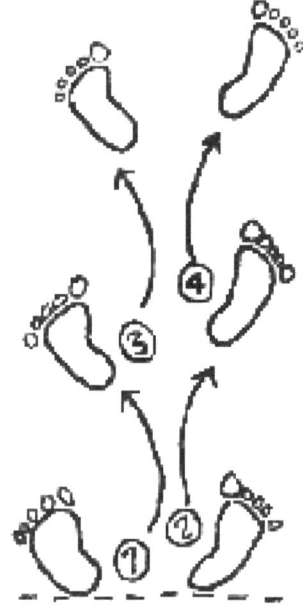

FIGURE 2 Zig-zag foot placement

There are a variety of suriashi exercises that illustrate movements a rikishi might have to perform in order to move his opponent out of the dohyo. Below is another movement illustrating movement around the edge of the dohyo:

Step 6

After the squat and push out of the first half of suriashi, return right arm with elbow pinned to side, forearm extended forward, and palms facing inward.

Raise left arm above shoulder with a semi-circle motion, elbow slightly bent toward forehead, palm facing outward.

Step 7

Slide left foot, then right foot, along edge of dohyo.

Continue around dohyo to starting point.

At end of exercise, twist at the hips, keep your upper arm in the same position, and extend the lower arm outward as if pushing opponent out of dohyo. Be sure to keep your feet planted inside the dohyo; do not take a step as you twist and push out.

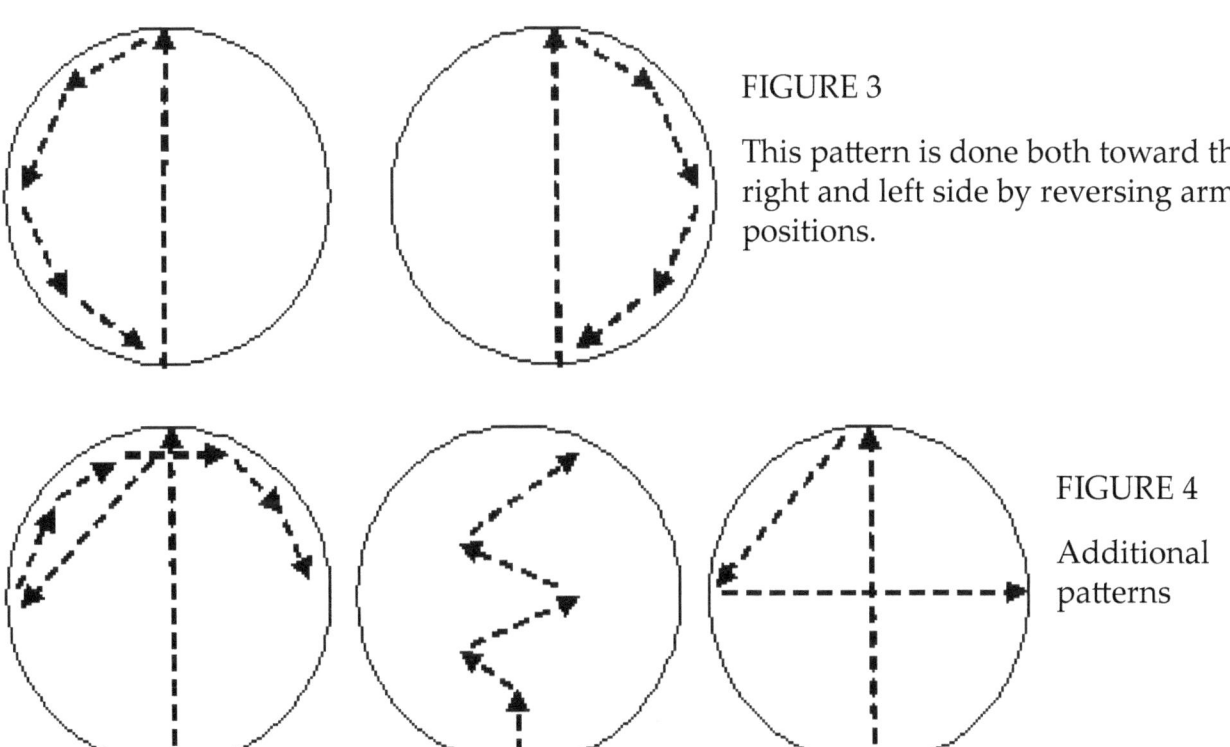

FIGURE 3

This pattern is done both toward the right and left side by reversing arm positions.

FIGURE 4

Additional patterns

UKEMI

Ukemi, a defensive position, is an indispensable and very important technique for protecting your own body. The reason for practicing ukemi is to protect your head and neck by teaching you how to fall properly. When you practice ukemi enough, it will become second-nature, and executing this move safely will help prevent many injuries over your career.

HOW TO PERFORM UKEMI WITH A PARTNER

Step 1

Place forehead on right or left side of defender's chest.

Step 2

Take a deep step forward with right leg. Defender pushes the shoulder with his hand to assist the motion.

Step 3

Roll onto the right or left shoulder.

Step 4

Roll with one continuous motion and get back on to your feet.

Step 5

Once standing, look at the defender and take the position of chugoshi.

Upon a signal from the defender, charge again, executing ukemi to the right or left.

Sumo Skills: Instructional Guide for Competitive Sumo

HOW TO PERFORM UKEMI WITHOUT A PARTNER

Step 1

Stand straight up.

Step 2

Take a step forward with the right (left) leg. Touch the dohyo with the right (left) hand.

This move can be executed to the right or left side. These are later referred to as "right (left)" in the text.

Step 3

Tuck chin into neck so head does not touch the dohyo.

Roll onto the right (left) shoulder—hand, elbow, and shoulder should touch the dohyo in that order.

Step 4

Look at stomach while rolling.

Roll with one continuous motion and get back onto your feet.

Step 5

Once standing, face toward the direction you just came from and take the position of chugoshi.

35

MATAWARI (KAIKYAKU)

The most important element in the development of physical strength for sumo is the flexibility of the body. Like training for the tachiai (initial charge), matawari is the most painful for rikishi who do not have a flexible body. Matawari is effective for developing flexibility of your hips but also for your whole body.

This routine should be completed after all other stretching exercises for maximum flexibility.

HOW TO PERFORM MATAWARI

Step 1

While sitting on the dohyo, spread both legs at an angle of 180 degrees, in basic terms—"do the splits."

Step 2

Grab right ankle with hands and touch chest to leg while keeping the leg straight—do not bend knee.

Alternate to each side—right and left leg.

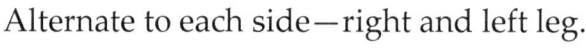

Stretch both sides slowly and firmly.

Step 3

Lean forward—stretch out arms 180 degrees and parallel with legs.

Keep leaning forward, touching the dohyo with head, shoulders/arms, chest, and stomach.

Stretch slowly and firmly.

Note: A beginner or someone who is not flexible may use a helper to push forward on the back.

TEPPO

Teppo is a basic movement of attack. It is a fundamental practice in which the balance and rhythm of the upper limbs and legs are required. Since it strengthens the back and upper body, it is directly useful for thrusting and pushing techniques.

HOW TO PERFORM TEPPO

Step 1

Lean on a pillar with both hands as in chugoshi position. Feet will be about one meter from pillar.

Step 2

Support with one hand and pull the other hand (elbow) backward.

Step 3

Slap the pole with the hand you just pulled back and take a step with the same side foot.

Step 4

Pull back the leg that stepped forward while pushing off the pillar with both hands.

Repeat with other side.

FROM SHIKIRI TO TACHIAI

These are the preparation movements at the beginning of a match which range from stillness to motion and combines technique, the mind, and the body at once. The rikishi places both hands on the dohyo, keeping in mind your opponent's readiness to start the match. The match will be signaled to begin by the referee (gyoji) when both athletes are still and all four hands are on the dohyo. Most bouts are won or lost at the moment of tachiai.

HOW TO PERFORM SHIKIRI TO TACHIAI

Step 1

Drop hips and center of gravity deep in a squat.

Place elbows on thighs of each leg.

Pull jaw toward neck but keep eyes up.

Shift force (weight) forward, but keep feet flat on dohyo.

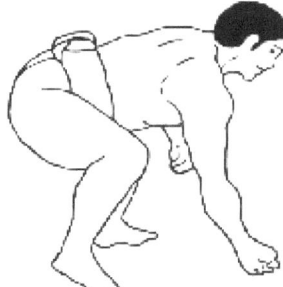

Step 2

Clench fist loosely and touch dohyo with pinky finger.

You may touch the dohyo with right or left hand.

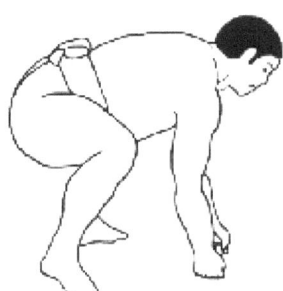

Step 3

Touch the dohyo with both hands.

Shift weight onto hands, still keeping feet flat on dohyo.

Hips should be lower than shoulder.

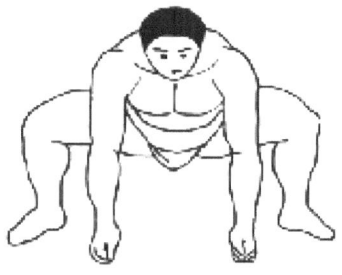

Step 4

Make initial charge with a push (oshi) and then take the position of chugoshi.

Chapter 5

BASIC SKILLS

There are basic skills used by both rikishi during the course of a sumo match. Mastery of these skills will give any rikishi a solid foundation and a strong edge over his opponent.

INITIAL CHARGE (TACHIAI)

The tachiai (initial charge) is probably the most important time of a sumo match. This is where a rikishi's preparation and actual combat meet. A sumo match is normally finished within a few seconds so it is imperative that a rikishi has a solid, strong start. A strong or weak tachiai usually is the difference between winning and losing.

HOW TO PERFORM TACHIAI AND BUTSUKARI—PUSH (OSHI) DRILL

Step 1

Charge against an opponent from the position of shikiri.

Defender opens chest so that he can be attacked easily.

From shikiri use the position of chugoshi to push.

Step 2

While striking opponent, place hands on bottom and side of his chest, under his armpits.

Bury forehead into upper chest. The forehead and hands should meet your defender at the same time for maximum impact.

Push opponent back and/or over with force.

Step 3

Push opponent with head and hands to the dohyo's edge.

Advance/slide your feet with suriashi.

Step 4

Force opponent out of the dohyo by squatting.

Come out of squat pushing forward and extending arms upward.

After forcing opponent out, squat at edge of dohyo.

Do not take a step forward; keep your feet anchored on the dohyo.

Step 5

Change directions and start again.

Step 6

Ukemi can be done in the middle and end of this training.

INITIAL CHARGE (TACHIAI) STYLES

As stated earlier, the tachiai is probably the most crucial aspect of a sumo match. This is where a rikishi's preparation and actual combat meet. It is imperative that a rikishi has a solid, strong start. A strong or weak tachiai usually is the difference between winning and losing.

This is the only time during a match that you have to *set up* a move or technique. Normally a match is over fairly quickly, so there is no time between movements to really set up for a certain technique. You have to be prepared to execute or defend against your opponent's attacks or defensive tactics spontaneously.

You will want to use different styles or techniques of tachiai depending on circumstances, such as various things about your opponent (size, strength, techniques they use, aggressiveness, etc.), injuries to yourself and your opponent, and typically, what feels natural or right to you at the time.

Some of these moves are actually winning techniques, while others are considered offensive moves but require another technique to win the match.

The best advice I can give you is this: KEEP MOVING (hopefully forward); do not give your opponent time to think.

VARIOUS STYLES OF THE INITIAL CHARGE (TACHIAI)

Figure 1

BUCHIKAMASHI

Charge in against an opponent with forehead and both hands, advance using suriashi and a pushing technique.

Figure 2

TAIATARI

Dash against opponent with shoulder and apply weight to drive him backward, securing grip on his mawashi.

Figure 3

KACHIAGE

Dash against opponent using upward arm movement to thrust near opponent's jaw.

Must be extremely quick in order to attack opponent before he comes out of shikiri position.

Figure 4

MAEMAWASHI-O-TORU

Charge against opponent, keeping low and grabbing front of mawashi.

Figure 5

OSODACHI

Charge later than your opponent so you can attack from under—and deflect—your opponent's charge.

Figure 6

OTTSUKERU

When your opponent attempts to take an inside grip or to thrust, you force the elbow of that arm from outside or under so that you defend against the attack.

Figure 7

HATAKIKOMU

Shift away from opponent's attack and use their momentum to push them down or out.

Figure 8

HIKKAKERU

Grab opponent's arm and turn away when opponent starts to use a thrusting technique.

Figure 9

SASHIMI

Take a step before opponent does so that you force opponent to lose balance when he is attempting to take a double inside grip.

Figure 10

HIPPARIKOMU

Tempt opponent, who is nimble and quick, in too close by spreading your arms out to pull opponent's inside arm into you.

Figure 11

TSUPPARI

Thrust opponent upward with a quick rotation of the arms and advance with suriashi.

NOTE: It is prohibited to continually tsuppari to the throat intentionally. (See "Prohibited Fouls and Techniques.")

Figure 12

NODOWA

Thrust upward at opponent's throat with the hand to raise his upper body, then continue forward by suriashi.

THRUST (TSUKI) TRAINING

A thrust (tsuki/tsuppari) is the technique in which a rikishi makes his opponent lose balance. The rikishi attacks his opponent's chest or shoulder with his palms, without grappling. This technique is best used when the rotation of quick thrusts with his arms coincides with the movement of his feet.

HOW TO PERFORM THRUST (TSUKI) TRAINING

Step 1

Charge from shikiri/tachiai position.

Thrust up on opponent's chest or shoulders.

Use quick rotation of both arms.

Step 2

Keep your jaw tucked to your chest.

Look at opponent with upward glance.

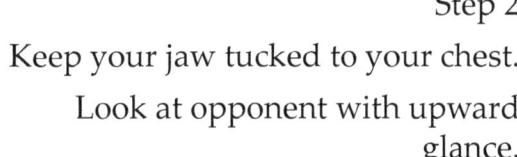

Step 3

Speed up the rotation of your arms.

Advance/slide your feet with suriashi.

Coordinate the movement of your arms and feet.

Step 4

When you force opponent to edge of dohyo, continue rotation of arms and take the position of chugoshi.

Be careful not to step out of dohyo before your opponent.

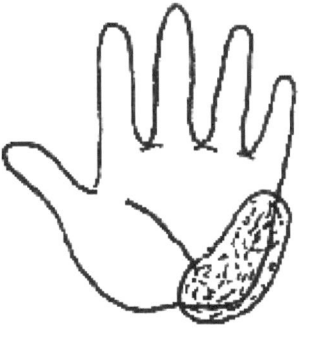

Figure 1

It is important to thrust with your wrists inside your elbows.

Use the little finger side of your palm; this is considered a power point. You do not use your fingers to thrust.

FORCE OUT (YORI) TRAINING

Yori can be done either gripping the mawashi or without gripping the mawashi. In either case, you cause your opponent to lose his balance and force him out of the dohyo.

This technique is best used when you can force your opponent out of the dohyo before your opponent grabs your mawashi.

VARIOUS SITUATIONS OF THE FORCE OUT (YORI)

Figure 1

Without gripping the mawashi.

Figure 2

Gripping the mawashi with one hand.

Figure 3

Gripping the mawashi with two hands.

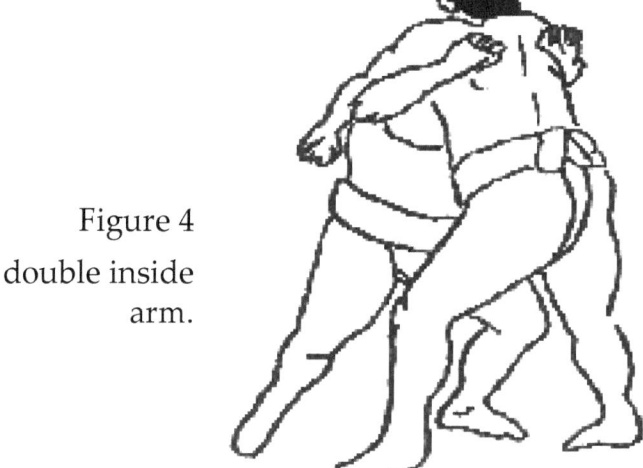

Figure 4

Using double inside arm.

DEFENSE (MAESABAKI) TRAINING

Maesabaki are not winning techniques, but various defensive techniques used to defend against an opponent's attack and then take a successful offensive position to control the match.

Maesabaki are several techniques used to obtain an advantageous position by using your arms to defend an opponent's attack. It is important that you close or tighten both sides so your opponent cannot take an inside grip.

VARIOUS SITUATIONS OF DEFENSE (MAESABAKI)

Figure 1

OTTSUKE

Fundamental move in which you prevent your opponent from taking an inside grip.

Attack by pushing upward with your palm placed on inner side of opponent's elbow and advance your feet forward using suriashi.

Figure 2

SHIBORIKOMI

Place your hand on opponent's elbow of inside arm; force elbow to the inside by closing your jaw to chin, arching your back.

Open stance of opposite foot and push opponent by turning upper body in that direction using force on his elbow.

Figure 3

MAKIKAESHI

Attempting to take a double inside grip or other favorite hold while grappling or while your opponent is also trying to take a grip.

Figure 4

HANEAGE

This technique is used to defend against an opponent's thrust.

It is best to push opponent's arm (near elbow) upward while opponent is thrusting. This raises opponent's center of gravity by *standing them up*.

Alternate technique is to block thrusting arm to the side.

Figure 5a - MAKIAGE 1

Figure 5b - MAKIAGE 2

Use this technique when holding your opponent's arm and he attempts to take an inside grip.

Place palm or hand on opponent's arm under bicep or elbow from the outside and push up.

Figure 6a - INASHI 1

Figure 6b - INASHI 2

In this technique you turn away from your opponent's push or thrust.

It is important not to let your opponent get behind you when you use this technique.

ADDITIONAL SKILLS

While this book does not contain all the styles, moves, or techniques available to a sumotori during a match, it does give you the basic tactics to try for control of the match's outcome. The following are some additional offensive and defensive tools to add to your arsenal.

ADDITIONAL OFFENSIVE AND DEFENSIVE TRAINING

BAR OPPONENT'S INSIDE ARM

Figure 1

When your opponent has an inside grip on your mawashi, grab that arm with both of yours, one around the forearm, the other at the elbow or above, then lift and straighten opponent's arm.

This should release the grip your opponent has, and you may throw your opponent down by swinging sideways while still clutching his arm.

Figure 2

When your opponent has a double inside grip, wrap each arm around his above the elbow and lift/straighten his arm.

HINT: To strengthen your hold, you may lock your fingers or hand and wrist together.

Again, this should release his grip, and you may force him out or throw him down by swinging sideways while clutching his arms.

BLOCK OPPONENT FROM GETTING HOLD OR GRIP

Figure 3

With one arm on inside, place under opponent's armpit, lift elbow, and turn forearm downward.

Figure 4

With both arms inside, place forehead on lower part of opponent's jaw, raise elbows, and turn forearms downward.

USING THE BODY

In sumo it is necessary to use your opponent's force against him before he executes a technique or to force your opponent to lose his balance. Therefore, it is important to know how to use your head, hips, arms, jaw, knees, shoulders, and wrists. You can improve your skill in sumo by using various parts of your body to help win matches.

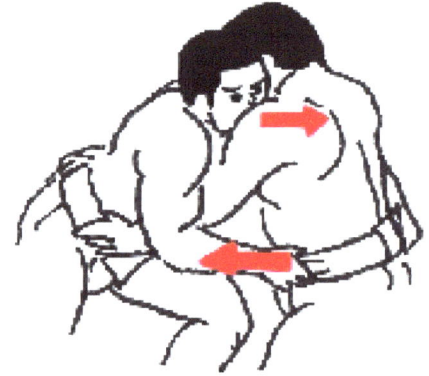

Figure 5

Push opponent's shoulder (upper body) with your head, using it as a fulcrum, while pulling his mawashi toward you.

An inside, front grip is the best position.

Figure 6a

You can weaken an opponent's strength and take an offensive position by placing your head on your opponent. By doing so you have an advantage and can force your opponent out more easily.

This is especially important for someone who is weaker or shorter.

Figure 6b

Figure 7

By using your shoulders you can lift your opponent's upper body and by doing so raise his center of gravity.

Raising your opponent's center of gravity allows a weaker/smaller wrestler to attack more easily.

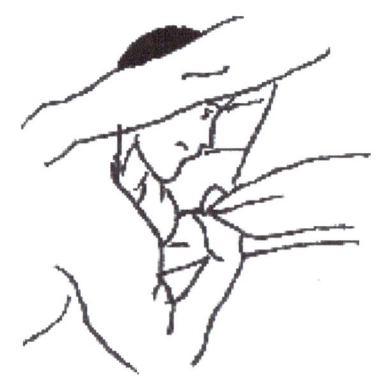

Figure 8

There are various ways in which you use your wrists during a match: grabbing the mawashi, pulling, throwing, and releasing the mawashi. It is especially important to use the wrists when pulling your opponent toward you when grabbing the front of his mawashi.

RELEASING OPPONENT'S GRIP ON MAWASHI

This technique is important because it allows you to defend against an opponent's attack and because the sudden release of your opponent's grip on your mawashi allows you to mount a surprise attack of your own.

Figure 9

When your opponent has an outside grip, place your hand under your opponent's armpit and your elbow on the inside of your opponent's arm.

Release his grip by driving your hips forward.

Figure 10

When your opponent has an inside grip and you have a grip on his mawashi, place your forearm/elbow on your opponent's wrist and throw your weight on it.

Release his grip by dropping the elbow down.

Figure 11

Release opponent's grip on the front of your mawashi before he puts his thumb in.

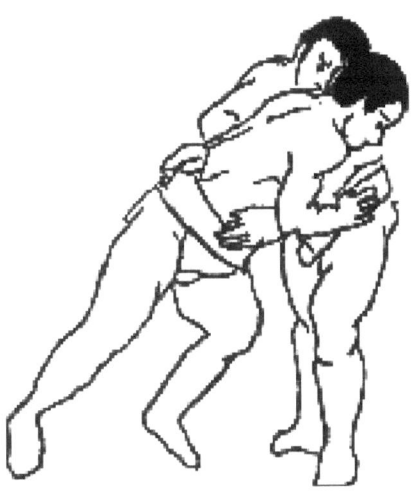

Figure 12

When your opponent has an inside grip, hold his gripping arm with your hand.

Release his grip by driving your hips forward while twisting.

Chapter 6

TECHNIQUES

INTRODUCTION TO TECHNIQUES

A sumo wrestling match may seem quite simple at first sight, just a couple big people belly bumping, but in reality, there is much more to it. The techniques used to win a match are complicated and varied. A sumotori usually specializes in one or two winning techniques (kimarite). But because many matches last only seconds and opponents do not want to cooperate, a wrestler is often required to use several techniques within a few compact moments.

A sumotori may maneuver his opponent to the dohyo's edge (tawara) with a belt grip. As he switches to a push attack trying to finish the match, his opponent—who failed with his initial thrusting—now suddenly feels free of his attacker's hold. His opponent grabs his mawashi in a last-ditch utchari attempt.

The combinations are infinite. It is often only in slow motion replays that we truly realize how intricate the sumotori's moves really were and what split-second timing was involved. The best wrestlers are quite naturally well-rounded; they have a varied technical arsenal, can think and react quickly, and also possess a strong fighting spirit.

Until 2001, there were 70 officially recognized winning techniques. In 2001, 12 winning techniques were added to the official list. All of these techniques involve various combinations of pushing, tugging, tripping, sweeping, tossing, throwing, and twisting.

The total of officially recognized winning techniques is now set at 82, although some connoisseurs go as far as to claim there are over 200. In the next few chapters we will cover default techniques (hizawa), prohibited fouls (kinjite), and all of the official techniques used by professional and amateur sumotori alike.

KEY ELEMENTS

There are three key elements to winning a match in sumo:

The first is being mentally prepared. Above all else, you have to know that you can and will win. If you go into a match thinking you don't have a chance, more often than not, you will meet your self-fulfilling prophecy. A successful sumotori has a warrior spirit. He must go into a match believing he can, and will, win—no matter who is on the other side. Most sumo matches last only a few seconds, so all you have to do is a couple quick things correctly and you can beat any opponent.

This leads us to the second most important element—technique. I've included this in the techniques chapter because it is so important that during keiko (practice) and while in combat you apply the proper posture, technique, and follow-up. If you don't attempt to be precise while doing shiko, suriashi, bustukari, etc. and while executing a technique during practice, it may very well translate to a loss during a match. Each of these movements is called fundamental because they are key to adding a victory to your win column. Each keiko movement and technique have particular movements and positioning that have been perfected over many years to help you WIN.

These first two ingredients are essential to you being successful in the dohyo. It doesn't matter what weight class you are in if you possess a warrior spirit and execute your movements skillfully. A smaller rikishi can and will beat a larger opponent if he has the will, knowledge, and ability to win.

This brings us to the third key component: physique. Your body type, build, shape, power, and/or size also play a factor in your aptitude to winning. If you ask most people, they would tend to say they would rather be on the heavier side of their weight class than on the lower-side. Size does matter, and this can be especially true when you are fighting a novice in the early stages of a sumo career. But once you start meeting opponents who are more technically proficient than you, your physique may not be the factor that it once was.

Remember that sumo is about balance and power. Sure, you can win by overpowering your opponent, but more often than not you win by harnessing your opponent's power and using it against him to offset his balance. You win by redirecting his power and movements in a way that maximizes your strengths and balance.

We call that KIMARITE (winning technique).

GUIDE TO UNDERSTANDING JAPANESE TERMINOLOGY

dashi = out of the dohyo (e.g., oshidashi, okuridashi, tsukidashi, tsuridashi, waridashi, shitatedashinage, uwatedashinage, kimedashi, okuritsuridashi)

gake = fall/trip (e.g., sotogake, uchigake, kawazugake)

hineri = twist or turn (e.g., kainahineri, kotehineri, shitatehineri, uwatehineri, gasshohineri, kubihineri)

nage = throw (e.g., kotonage, shitatenage, shitatedashinage, sukuinage, uwatenage, uwatedashinage, kakenage, koshinage, kubinage, nichonnage, okurinage, harimanage, tsukaminage, yaguranage, tokkurinage)

okuri = behind or rear (e.g., okuridashi, okurinage, okurihikiotoshi, okuritaoshi, okuritsuridashi, okurigake, okuritsuriotoshi)

oshi = push or force out without grip on mawashi (continued pressure) (e.g., oshidashi, oshitaoshi)

otoshi = push/fall forward onto the dohyo (e.g., tsukiotoshi, hikiotoshi, makiotoshi, okurihikiotoshi, okubiotoshi, tsuriotoshi, okuritsuriotoshi)

shitate = underarm or inside (e.g., shitatenage, shitatehineri, shitatedashinage)

soto = outside (e.g., sotogake, sotokomata, sotomuso, sototassukizori)

taoshi = push/fall back onto the dohyo (e.g., yoritaoshi, oshitaoshi, abisetaoshi, kimetaoshi, okuritaoshi, tsukitaoshi)

tsuki = thrust (not continued pressure) (e.g., tsukite, tsukidashi, tsukitaoshi, tsukiotoshi, tsukihiza)

tsuri = lift or raise (e.g., tsuridashi, tsuriotoshi, okuritsuridashi, okuritsuriotoshi)

uchi = inside (e.g., uchigake, uchimuso)

uwate = overhand, outside, or over the shoulder (e.g., uwatenage, uwatedashinage, uwatehineri)

yori = push out holding the mawashi (e.g., yorikiri, yoritaoshi)

zori = backward body drop (e.g., zori, kakezori, shumokuzori, sototasukizori, tasukizori, tsutaezori)

TECHNIQUE SIMILARITY LIST

Listed below are the 82 winning techniques grouped into similar types. As your training becomes more advanced, you may want to review techniques that are similar so that you can be familiar with what options you may have available during a match, both offensively and defensively.

KEY: **Frequent**, **Common**, **Uncommon**, **Rare**

Throw:
>Katasukashi, Kotenage, Shitatenage, Sukuinage, Uwatenage, Uwatedashinage,
>Kakenage, Koshinage, Kubinage, Nichonage, Okurinage, Shitatedashinage, Tottari,
>Amiuchi, Harimanage, Kawazugake, Tsukaminage, Yaguranage, Yobimodoshi,
>Ipponzeoi, Sakatottari, Tokkurinage

Twist:
>Utchari,
>Kainahineri, Kirikaeshi, Kotehineri, Makiotoshi, Shitatehineri, Uchimuso, Uwatehineri,
>Gasshohineri, Kubihineri, Nimaigeri, Osakate, Sotomuso,

Push / Force Out:
>Yorikiri, Yoritaoshi, Oshidashi, Oshitaoshi, Okuridashi,
>Abisetaoshi, Okuritaoshi, Ushiromotare, Waridashi, Watashikome,
>Mitokorozeme, Sabaori,

Thrust:
>Tsukidashi, Tsukiotoshi,
>Tsukitaoshi

Sweep / Trip:
>Sotogake, Uchigake,
>Kakenage, Kekaeshi, Ketaguri, Kirikaeshi, Susoharai,
>Chongake, Kawazugake, Mitokorozeme, Nimaigiri,
>Okurigake

Leg Lift:
>Ashitori, Komatasukui, Susotori,
>Kozumatori, Mitokorozeme, Omata, Sotokomata, Sotomuso, Yaguranage,
>Tsumatori

Arm-Bar:
   Kimedashi, Kotenage,

   Kimetaoshi, Kotehineri, Tottari,

   Amiuchi, Chongake

   Sakatottari (Defense against arm-bar)

Head:
   Kubinage, Sokubiotoshi,

   Gasshohineri, Kubihineri, Zubuneri,

   Tokkurinage

Slap / Pull Down:
   Hatakikomi, Hikiotoshi,

   Hikkake, Kainahineri, Okurihikiotoshi, Sokubiotoshi,

   Sabaori, Yobimodoshi

Lift:
   Tsuridashi, Utchari,

   Okuritsuridashi,

   Tsukaminage, Tsuriotoshi,

   Okuritsuriotoshi

From Behind or Side:
   Okuridashi,

   Kirikaeshi, Okurihikiotoshi, Okurinage, Okuritaoshi, Okuritsuridashi,

   Sotokomata,

   Okurigake, Okuritsuriotoshi, Tsumatori

Defense for Behind or Side:
   Ushiromotare,

   Kawazugake, Sotomuso,

   Ipponzeoi

82 Winning Techniques

5	4	16	31		19	12
Default	Bread & Butter	Most Frequent	Common		Uncommon	Rare
Fumidashi	Yorikiri	Hatakikomi	Abisetaoshi	Okurihikiotoshi*	Amiuchi	Ipponzeoi
Isamiashi	Yoritaoshi	Hikiotoshi	Ashitori	Okurinage*	Chongake	Izori
Koshikudake	Oshidashi	Katasukashi	Hikkake	Okuritaoshi	Gasshohineri	Kakezori
Tsukihiza	Oshitaoshi	Kimedashi	Kainahineri	Okuritsuridashi*	Harimanage	Okurigake*
Tsukite		Kotenage	Kakenage	Shitatedashinage	Kawazugake	Okuritsuriotoshi*
		Okuridashi	Kekaeshi	Shitatehineri	Kozumatori*	Sakatottari
		Shitatenage	Ketaguri	Sokubiotoshi*	Kubihineri	Shumokuzori
		Sotogake	Kimetaoshi	Susoharai	Mitokorozeme	Sototasukizori
		Sukuinage	Kirikaeshi	Susotori	Nimaigeri	Tasukizori
		Tsukidashi	Komatasukui	Tottari	Omata	Tokkurinage*
		Tsukiotoshi	Koshinage	Tsukitaoshi	Osakate*	Tsumatori
		Tsuridashi	Kotehineri*	Uchimuso	Sabaori	Tsutaezori*
		Uchigake	Kubinage	Ushiromotare*	Sotokomata	
		Utchari	Makiotoshi	Uwatehineri	Sotomuso	
		Uwatedashinage	Nichonage	Waridashi	Tsukaminage	
		Uwatenage		Watashikome	Tsuriotoshi	
					Yaguranage	
					Yobimodoshi	
					Zubuneri	

*The 12 techniques added to the Japanese official list of winning techniques in 2001

DEFAULT TECHNIQUES (HIWAZA)

Default techniques are, as the name suggests, not really techniques at all, but an unfortunate act or reaction by your opponent. As the attacker, you do not do anything in particular to cause your opponent to fall, touch down, or step out. However, you do get credit in the *win* column. These five (5) defaults are listed outside the official list of winning techniques.

FUMIDASHI

Rear Step Out

A rikishi accidentally steps back over the edge without his opponent initiating any kind of technique.

ISAMIASHI

Forward Step Out

An attacking rikishi accidentally steps too far forward and out of the ring before winning the match, giving the victory to his opponent.

KOSHIKUDAKE

Inadvertent Collapse

A rikishi falls over backward without his opponent attempting any technique, often the result of a rikishi overcommitting to an attack.

TSUKIHIZA

Knee Touch Down

A rikishi stumbles without any real contact with his opponent and loses by touching down with one or both knees.

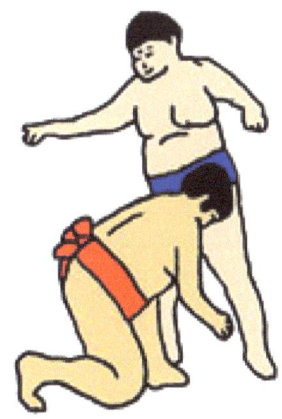

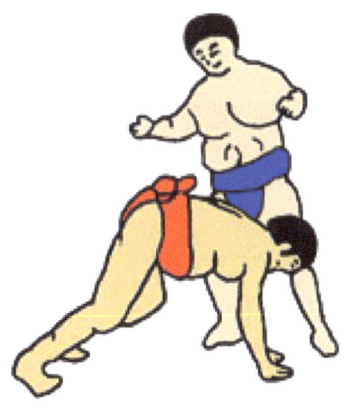

TSUKITE

Hand Touch Down

A rikishi stumbles without any real contact with his opponent and loses by touching down with one or both hands.

ADDITIONAL RULES

KABAITE

Opponent Already Defeated

If you are falling simultaneously with your opponent and he is determined (by the gyoji) to already be defeated (shinitai), and you touch the ground before he does in order to protect him from injury, the gyoji may rule in your favor. This is called kabaite.

TSUKITAI

Opponent Not Yet Defeated

If you are falling simultaneously with your opponent and he is determined (by the gyoji) to not yet be defeated (ikitai), and you touch the ground before he does, the gyoji will rule in favor of your opponent. This is called tsukitai.

PROHIBITED FOULS (KINJITE)

The following prohibited fouls will result in a disqualification and loss of the match:

- Hitting with a closed fist
- Pulling opponent's hair
- Jabbing at opponent's eyes or solar plexus
- Biting
- Grabbing or pulling the groin area
- Grabbing the throat
- Kicking at the chest or waist
- Bending back opponent's fingers
- Slapping opponent's face with arm outstretched more than shoulder width
- Taking hold of clothing other than the mawashi (e.g., underpants, leotard, bandages, support pads, etc.) twice or more

MOST FREQUENTLY USED TECHNIQUES

This section is the meat of sumo. The following techniques are the most frequently used methods of winning a match by professional and amateur sumotori alike.

Most likely this will be the group of techniques you will learn to use first and the group most used against you.

Bread & Butter Techniques

These are the four (4) core techniques that your training regimen will be focused on. Utilizing your training will help you win your match. Remember, most matches last less than 10 seconds. More than 50% of the techniques that lead to a win are among these four core techniques.

Yorikiri	Force Out
Yoritaoshi	Force Down
Oshidashi	Push Out
Oshitaoshi	Push Down

16 Other Most Frequent Techniques

Hatakikomi	Slap Down
Hikiotoshi	Pull Down
Tsukidashi	Thrust Out
Tsukiotoshi	Thrust Down Forward
Uwatenage	Overarm Throw
Uwatedashinage	Pulling Overarm Throw
Sotogake	Outside Leg Trip
Uchigake	Inside Leg Trip
Katasukashi	Shoulder Swing Down
Kimedashi	Arm Bar Force Out
Kotenage	Arm Throw
Okuridashi	Rear Push Out
Shitatenage	Underarm Throw Down
Sukuinage	Beltless Arm Throw
Tsuridashi	Lift Out
Utchari	Pivot Throw

YORIKIRI

Force Out

Original 70: Yes

The attacker drives his opponent backward and out of the ring, maintaining a grip on the opponent's mawashi at all times.

YORIKIRI

Force Out

Step 1

Grab your opponent's mawashi from the inside and pull in the direction of that grip. The technique works best when you push with your outside grip/arm and pull in the direction of your inside grip. Always maintain your center of gravity lower than your opponent.

Step 2

Pull your opponent into you by gripping his mawashi and raising your opponent's hip. This allows you to keep your center of gravity lower than his.

Step 3

If you are powerful enough to heave your opponent out of the dohyo that is as effective as driving your opponent back and out of the dohyo.

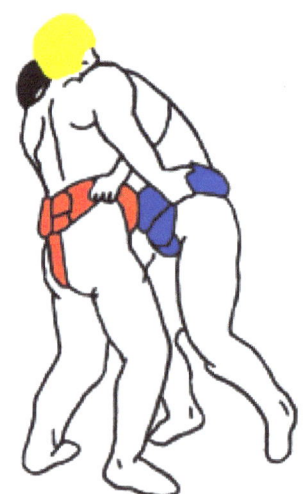

YORITAOSHI

Force Down

Original 70: Yes

The opponent is driven backward and collapses under the force of the attack. The attacker must maintain some grip on his opponent's mawashi. Same as yorikiri except that the opponent is forced off his feet.

YORITAOSHI

Force Down

Step 1

Grab your opponent's mawashi from the inside and pull in the direction of that grip. The technique works best when you push with your outside grip/arm and pull in the direction of your inside grip. Always maintain your center of gravity lower than your opponent.

Step 2

Pull your opponent into you by gripping his mawashi and raising your opponent's hip. This allows you to keep your center of gravity lower than his.

Step 3

When your opponent is driven backward under the force of the attack, it is called yoritaoshi.

OSHIDASHI

Push Out

Original 70: Yes

The attacker pushes his opponent out of the ring without gripping the mawashi. Unlike a frontal thrust out (tsukidashi), the attacker must maintain hand contact at all times.

OSHIDASHI

Push Out

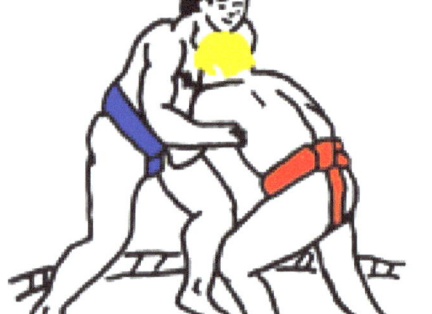

Step 1

If executed properly, your opponent will not be able to defend himself in any way. Oshi (pushing) is the most basic technique and is the secret to winning in sumo.

Drop your body and bury your head into your opponent's chest and pushing him upward.

Step 2

Attack immediately after the tachiai (initial charge) with a quick forward shuffle of your feet.

Step 3

To ensure your win, drive your opponent out of the dohyo by dropping your hips and extending your arms when your opponent is at the edge.

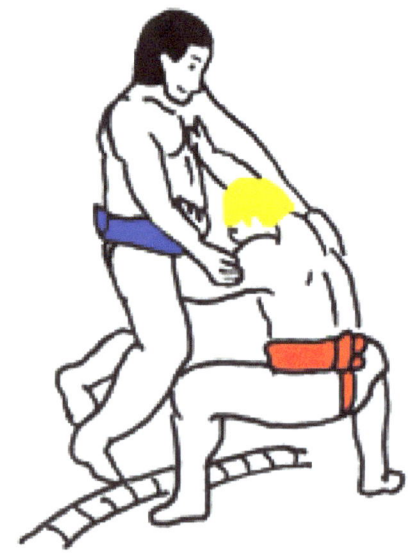

OSHITAOSHI

Push Down

Original 70: Yes

Similar to tsukitaoshi (thrust down backward), the attacker pushes his opponent backward and then over. Also very similar to oshidashi, but your opponent falls backward onto the dohyo from your pushing.

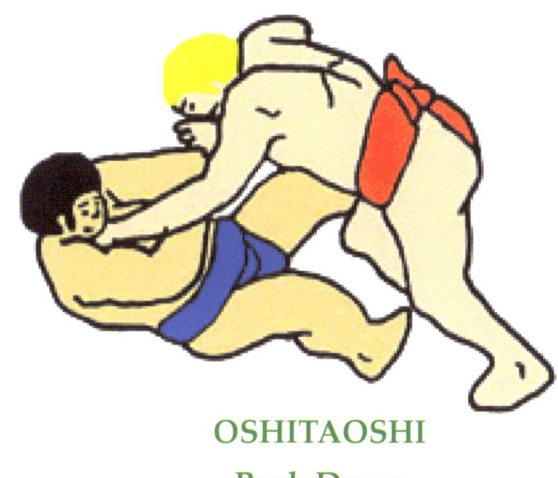

OSHITAOSHI

Push Down

Step 1

Drop your body and bury your head into your opponent's chest and then push him upward.

Step 2

Attack immediately after the tachiai (initial charge) with a quick forward shuffle of your feet.

Step 3

Drop your hips and extend your arms and cause your opponent to lose his balance and fall down backward from your intense pushing.

HATAKIKOMI

Slap Down

Original 70: Yes

Often seen at the tachiai, the attacker shifts away from opponent's charges and slaps the opponent's shoulder, back, or arm with one or both hands, directing him down, and forcing him to touch the ground with one or both hands. This can also be used during a heated thrust exchange.

HATAKIKOMI
Slap Down

Step 1

This is best used when you have raised your opponent up with a thrusting technique. When your opponent charges in with his head low, slap down his shoulder or back.

Step 2

As you slap down your opponent's shoulders or back, side step his charge, and use his momentum to push him down and force him to continue on past you. If you do not step to the side, he will come directly into you and possibly catch himself and force you out before he falls to the ground.

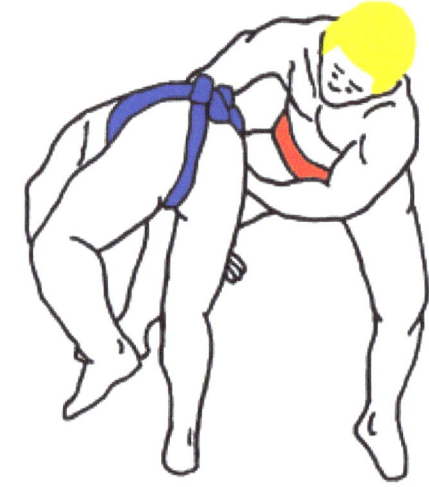

Step 3

Follow through by continuing to slap down your opponent's shoulders or back to be sure that his hand(s) have touched the dohyo, he has fallen down, or he has continued out of the ring.

FREQUENT

HIKIOTOSHI

Pull Down

Original 70: Yes

Similar to hatakikomi, the attacker pulls the opponent down while backing away and pulling on the arm, shoulder, or front of the opponent's mawashi.

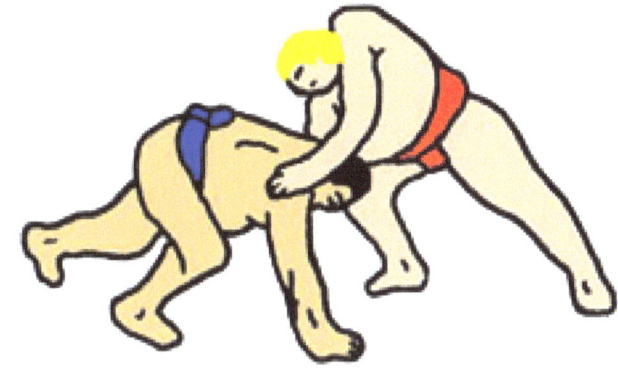

HIKIOTOSHI
Pull Down

Step 1

When your opponent is pushing against you, slap down his arm or grab an arm and pull him down and toward you, causing him to lean forward. This technique can also be used as soon as you and your opponent charge in together (not necessarily during the tachiai).

Step 2

As your opponent comes toward you, take a step backward and to the side while you pull down on the front of his mawashi and/or slap down his shoulder or back.

Step 3

Pull down your opponent rather than slap him down by twisting away from him while pulling him down. If you have a grip on his mawashi, do not twist, just pull his hips down and he will fall.

TSUKIDASHI

Thrust Out

Original 70: Yes

The attacker drives his opponent backward and over the edge with a sustained tsuppari or rhythmical thrusting motion. Unlike oshidashi (push out), the attacker does not have to maintain hand contact at all times.

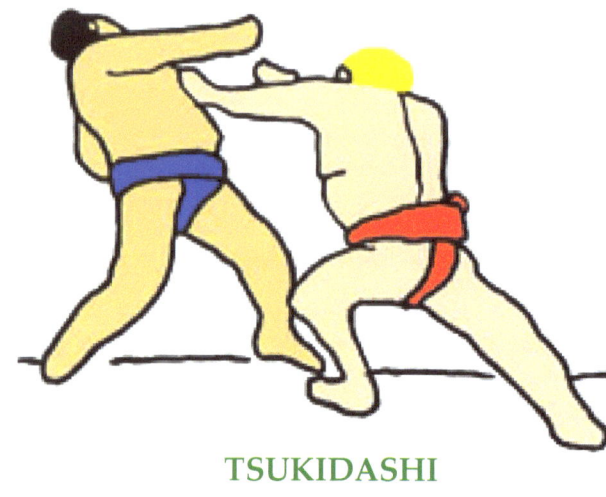

FREQUENT

TSUKIDASHI
Thrust Out

Step 1

Tsuki (thrusting) is one of the basic techniques in sumo, like yori (force out) and oshi (pushing).

The key to this technique is to maintain a continuous, quick rotation of thrusts from both hands. It is important to pull back on your thrusting arm quickly and slide/step forward from the same side as your thrusting arm.

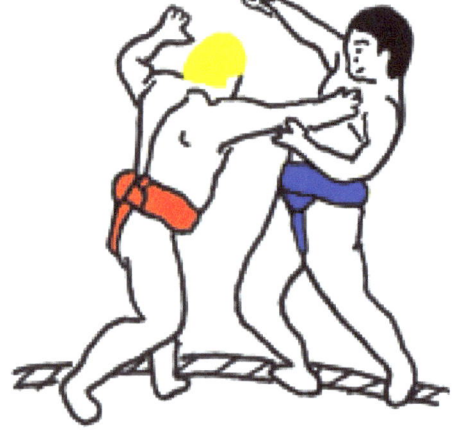

Step 2

Thrust at your opponent's chest from the inside with the palm of your hand, not your fingers.

Step 3

Drive your opponent out of the dohyo, using your full body weight, behind your powerful arm thrusts, in an upward motion.

TSUKIOTOSHI

Thrust Down Forward

Original 70: Yes

The attacker drives his opponent down into the clay with a thrusting motion after placing his open hand on the opponent's shoulder/shoulder blade. This is often used as a last-ditch effort at the edge.

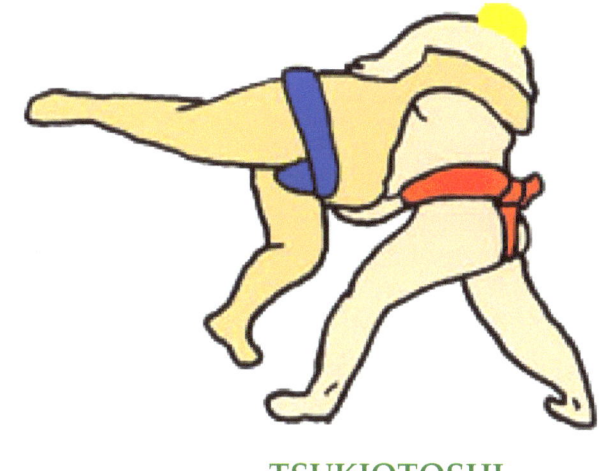

TSUKIOTOSHI

Thrust Down Forward

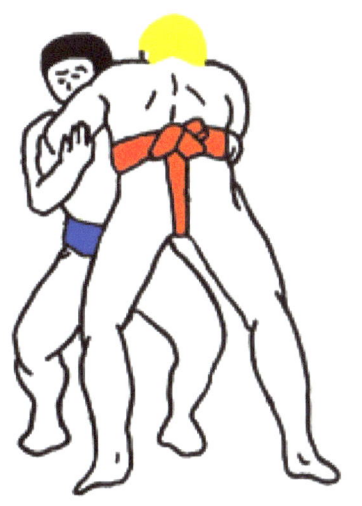

Step 1

During a heated pushing exchange, this technique is best used when your opponent launches his counterattack. When he starts to push, place your outside hand on his shoulder/shoulder blade.

Step 2

Pivot one deep step backward to avoid his pushing and slap/push your opponent downward.

Step 3

This technique is usually done when driven to the edge of the dohyo. When executed successfully, your opponent falls down on both hands. Skillful footwork is essential.

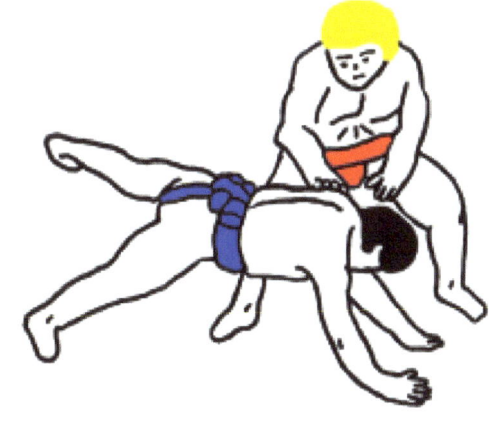

UWATENAGE

Overarm Throw

Original 70: Yes

This technique is the foundation of throwing and is the most common throwing technique.

After establishing an outside grip on the mawashi, the attacker throws his opponent by heaving him down at a sharp angle as he turns away, twisting his hip under his opponent and leaning forward, throwing him down.

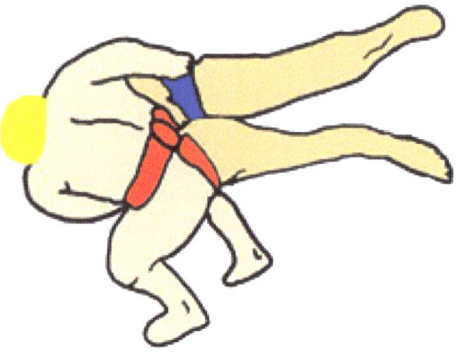

UWATENAGE

Overarm Throw

Step 1

Position your jaw on your opponent's neck or shoulder and pull your opponent into you with an inside grip.

Step 2

Throw your opponent down using your outside grip as you twist.

Step 3

Keep turning away from your opponent, twisting him around your body and pushing him downward. Be sure to maintain your own balance and keep your center of gravity low.

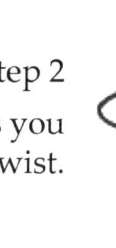

Figure 1

Movement of your feet while performing uwatenage

UWATEDASHINAGE

Pulling Overarm Throw

Original 70: Yes

UWATEDASHINAGE
Pulling Overarm Throw

From an outside grip, the attacker pulls his opponent forward and down as he turns away. The major difference between this technique and uwatenage (overarm throw) is the forward pull. Sometimes the only clear difference between these two techniques is that the sumotori are much closer during uwatenage, which makes more use of the power in the arms and body, then in uwatendashinage where the bodies are farther apart and power comes from the wrist.

When you pull your opponent forward and out with an outside grip, it is uwatedashinage; if you do it with an inside grip, it is shitatedashinage.

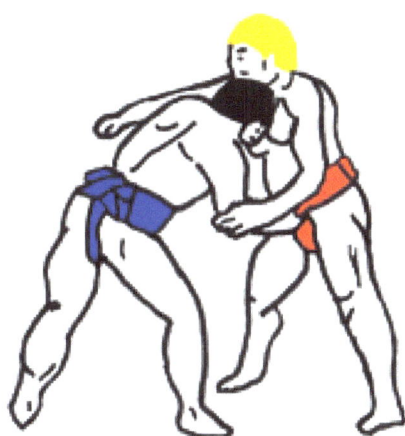

Step 1

Notice when your opponent is turned a little sideways to you; this technique can be easily used in this position.

Step 2

Pull your opponent with an outside grip in the direction his knees are turned. Use your other arm to pull your opponent's head down and forward. With the outside grip you can turn away from him easily and lock up his inside arm with your elbow.

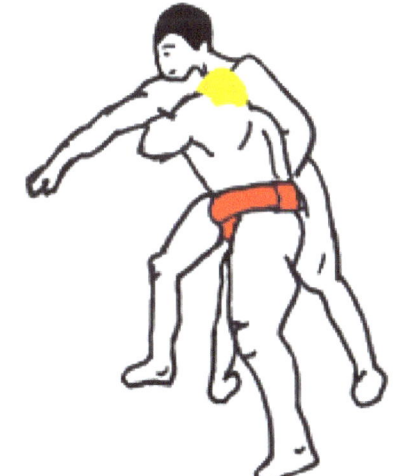

Step 3

It is important to not allow your opponent to take an outside grip on your mawashi.

The throw is successfully accomplished when you are centered on his body which is turned sideways.

SOTOGAKE

Outside Leg Trip

Original 70: Yes

The attacker pulls his opponent into him and hooks the opponent's lead leg from the outside, driving him over backward. Similar to uchigake, which is an inside leg trip. Best used by a taller rikishi on a shorter one.

SOTOGAKE
Outside Leg Trip

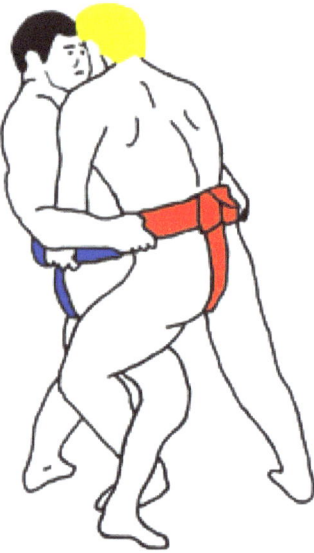

Step 1

Pull your opponent into you with a double grip on his mawashi and hook your lower leg around his leg.
This move is best executed if you hook the same leg as your inside grip.

Step 2

Lean into your opponent while maintaining your grip on his mawashi and hooking his leg.

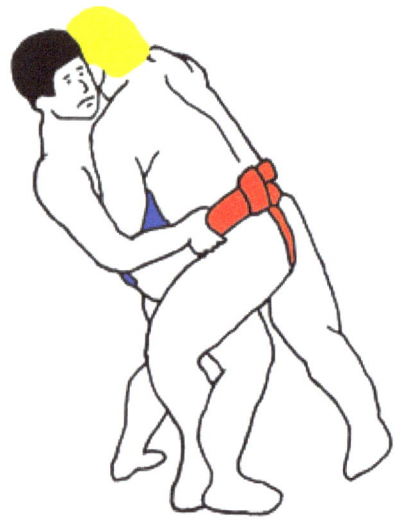

Step 3

Force your opponent over backward by leaning your upper body into him. If you had a grip on his mawashi from the rear, be sure to move your grip to the side or front as you fall on top of him/her.

UCHIGAKE

Inside Leg Trip

Original 70: Yes

As the attacker pulls his opponent forward, he hooks the opponent's lead leg from the inside. He then pulls the opponent's leg out from under him, pulling with a circular motion, as he drives him over onto his back. To make the throw effective, the leg must be twisted around at the lowest possible point of the opponent's leg. Used by a smaller rikishi on a larger or stronger one.

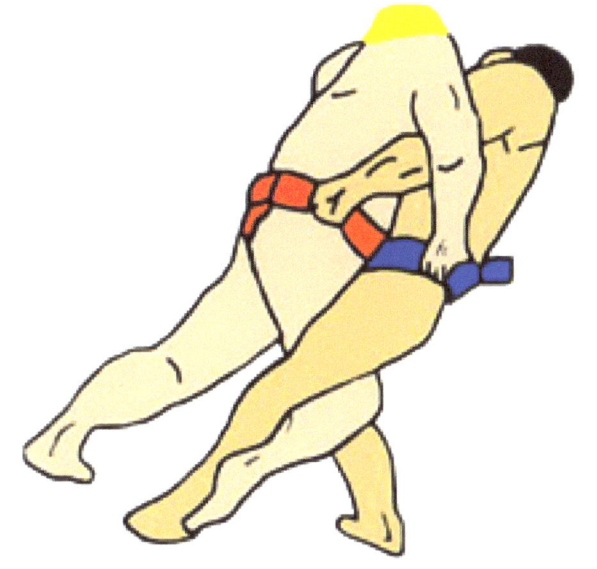

UCHIGAKE
Inside Leg Trip

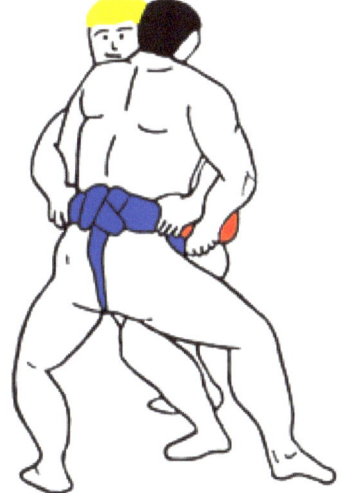

Step 1

Pull your opponent into you either with a grip on his mawashi or by initiating a throw. When he steps forward, hook your leg inside his. This move is executed better if you hook the same side as your inside grip.

Hook your opponent's leg as low as possible on his lead leg. As you sweep his leg out, draw a circle with your hooking leg.

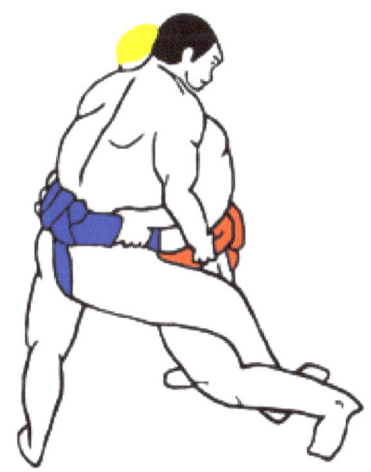

Step 2

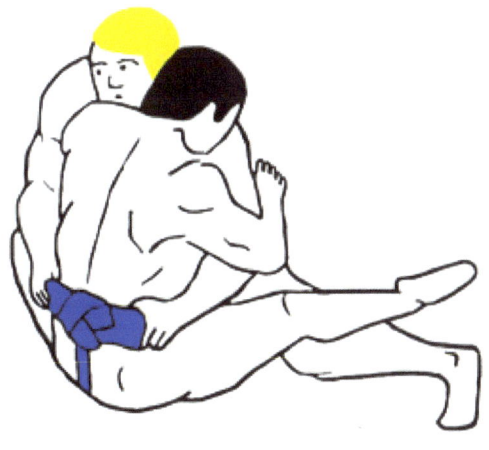

Step 3

Lean into your opponent with your upper body and continue to pull him toward you, forcing him over backward.

KATASUKASHI

Shoulder Swing Down

Original 70: Yes

The attacker forces his opponent down by placing one hand on the opponent's shoulder blade from the inside and one from the outside, pulling him down and forward. This move is best used when your opponent charges in with his head low.

KATASUKASHI
Shoulder Swing Down

Step 1

With one arm/hand hooking or holding your opponent's armpit, place your other hand over your opponent on his shoulder blade as he launches a counter-push technique.

Step 2

Turn away from your opponent while pulling him.

Step 3

Pull him down and forward while slapping your opponent's shoulder with the other hand.

KIMEDASHI

Arm Bar Force Out

Original 70: Yes

The attacker locks up the defender's elbows by wrapping his own arms around them from the outside and pulling up and in to march or swing the opponent backward and out of the ring.

KIMEDASHI

Arm Bar Force Out

Step 1

Use this technique when your opponent has two inside grips or there is a height and strength difference between you and your opponent.

Lock up your opponent's two arms (inside yours) with outside grips so that he cannot move. Pull up on his arms.

Step 2

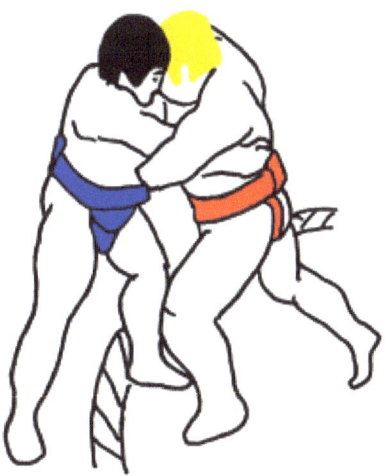

Step 3

Force your opponent back and out of the dohyo. Do not weaken your grip until he is out of the ring.

FREQUENT

KOTENAGE

Arm Throw

Original 70: Yes

The attacker wraps his arm around the opponent's inside gripping arm, locking it up on or near the elbow and turning away from him, usually at the edge of the ring. Similar in principle to uwatenage except that the mawashi is not used.

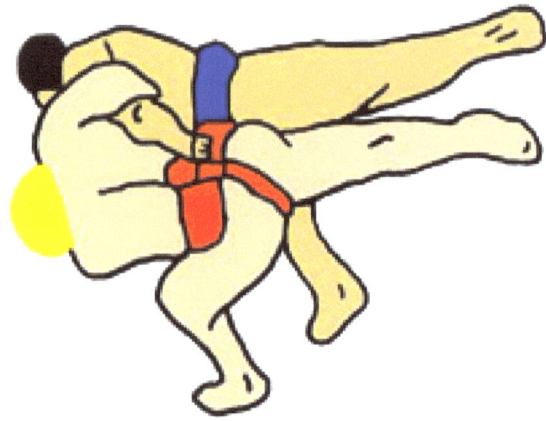

KOTENAGE

Arm Throw

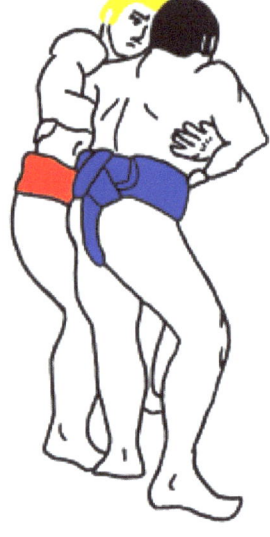

Step 1

Often used as a last-ditch attempt at the edge of the dohyo but it is also effective when your opponent charges hard at the tachiai. Wrap your arm around your opponent's arm from the outside and turn away.

Step 2

While turning away, lock up your opponent's inside arm near the elbow.

Step 3

Force your opponent down by leaning forward and twisting his arm downward.

OKURIDASHI

Rear Push Out

Original 70: Yes

The attacker drives his opponent out from behind.

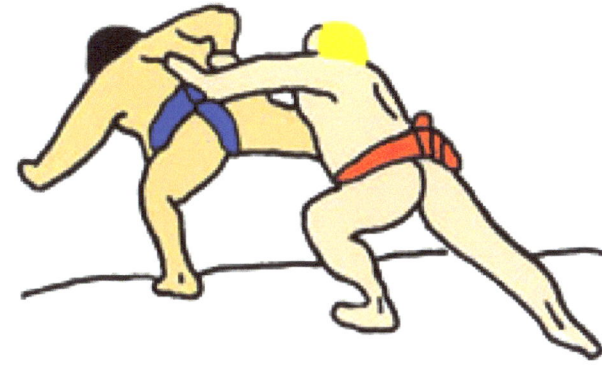

OKURIDASHI

Rear Push Out

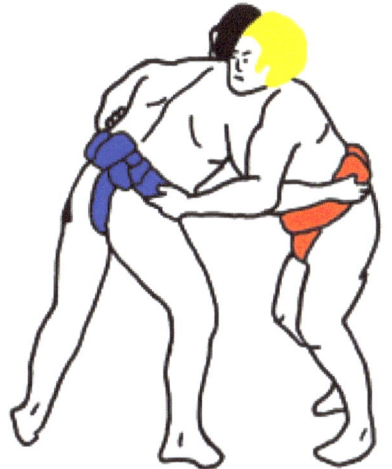

Step 1

Use this technique when your opponent is pushing or thrusting you and use his power and momentum against him.

Step 2

Best used when you grab your opponent's mawashi and turn away by taking a step to the side and pulling him so that you are to his side or in back of him.

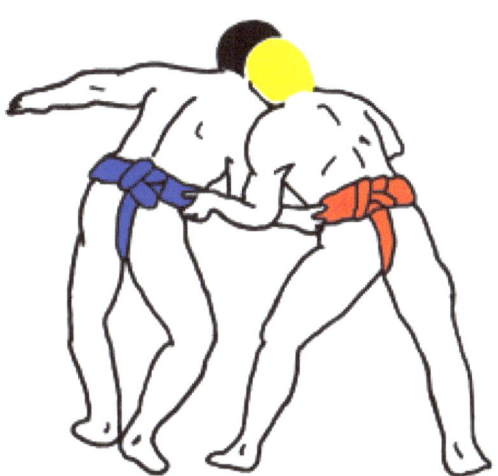

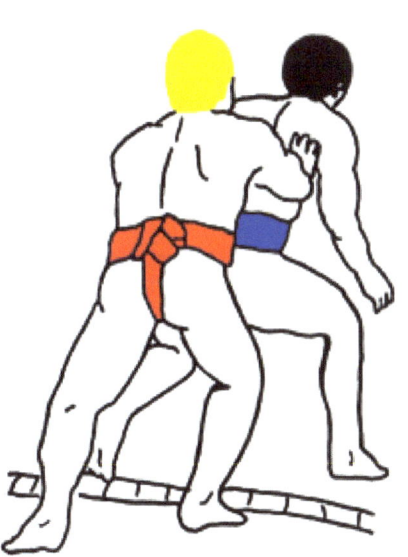

Step 3

Continue pulling/pushing your opponent from behind and out of the dohyo.

SHITATENAGE

Underarm Throw Down

Original 70: Yes

One of the most common throwing techniques, the attacker pulls straight down with his inside gripping hand as he turns away from his opponent.

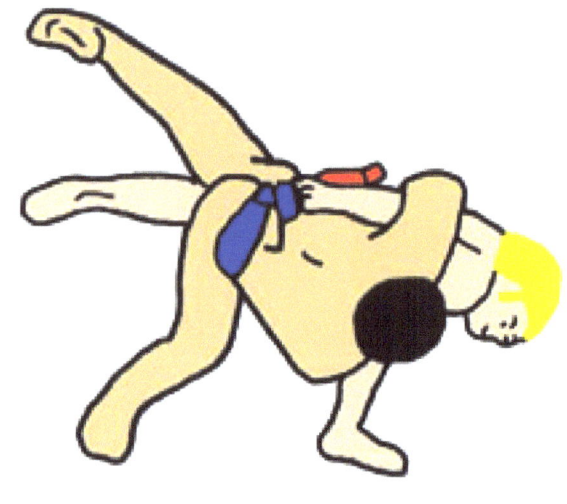

SHITATENAGE
Underarm Throw Down

Step 1
This technique is usually not done as the main attack but is accomplished when your opponent reacts to an immediate prior attack.

Step 2
Turn away from your opponent and lift him with your inside elbow. Your leg should be positioned inside his.

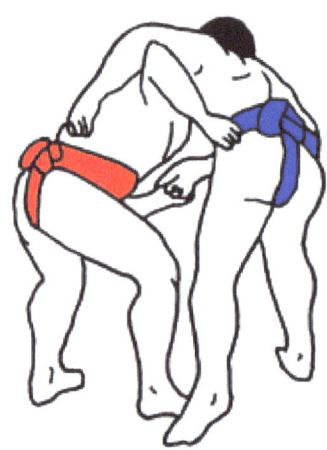

Step 3
Continue to turn away from him. Lift your inside leg to cause your opponent to become off balance.

Step 4
If your opponent is trying to use uwatenage at the same time, the one whose center of gravity is lower and more stable will win the match.

SUKUINAGE

Beltless Arm Throw

Original 70: Yes

From an inside gripping position, the attacker releases the gripping hand and extends that inside arm across his opponent's back as he turns away and pulls the opponent forward and down. The attacker's hip is shifted under his opponent's body and then the twisting throw is executed with no grip on the mawashi.

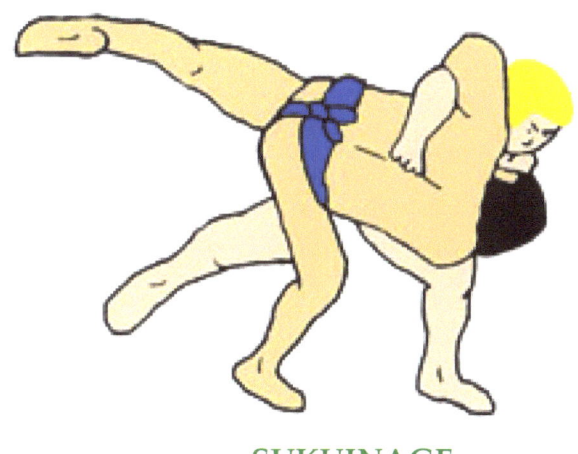

SUKUINAGE

Beltless Arm Throw

FREQUENT

Step 1

Extend an inside arm across your opponent's back. Use your other hand to grab his upper arm/elbow and twist him around and down. To be effective, force your inside arm down and take a deep step in the direction of the inside arm.

This throw is done occasionally from a double inside arm.

Step 2

As you turn away or twist, place your hip into your opponent to use as a trip. Your foot remains on the dohyo. Be sure to lock your opponent's inside arm at the elbow by grabbing it with the palm of your hand.

Step 3

Continue to rotate him around your hip and down to finish the bout.

TSURIDASHI

Lift Out

Original 70: Yes

This power technique can be executed from either a single or double inside grip, or even a double outside grip. The attacker takes hold of the opponent's mawashi, drops his hips, and heaves his opponent into the air, lifting him over and out of the ring. Occasionally, it is done without gripping the mawashi. This technique requires great skill in getting both hands on the mawashi and tremendous strength in lifting out.

TSURIDASHI
Lift Out

Step 1

Pull your opponent toward you and lower your hips so that your mawashi is lower than your opponent's.

Step 2

Lift your opponent into the air. Do not let him separate your upper bodies. Pull/keep his mawashi in tight to yours.

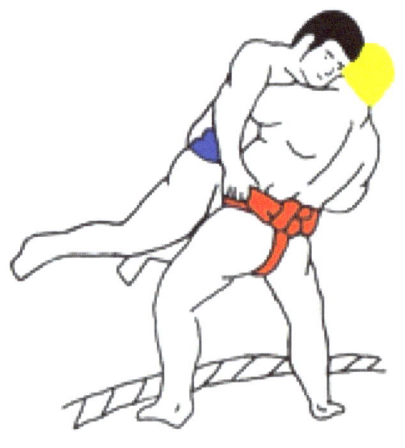

Step 3

Carry your opponent sideways (in order to keep your balance) to the edge of the dohyo and set him down outside the ring.

Note: When performing tsuridashi (or similar lifting technique, e.g., okuritsuridashi), you are allowed to step one foot out of the dohyo and place your opponent on the ground. You must have full control of your opponent and step out forward, not sideways or backward. This is done for safety to prevent injury to either rikishi. The match is over as soon as you step out, before you place your opponent on the ground.

UTCHARI

Pivot Throw

Original 70: Yes

In this last-ditch effort to win after being driven to the edge, the attacker drops his hips while pulling his opponent up and past him. The attacker is quite often forced over onto his back, but the twisting motion of his hips forces his opponent to touch down a fraction of a second before he does. A spectacular and crowd-pleasing throw which turns apparent defeat into sudden victory.

UTCHARI

Pivot Throw

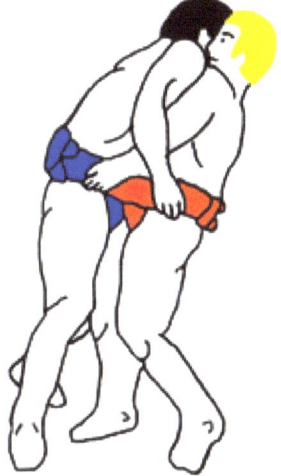

Step 1

When driven to the edge, drop your hips, lean backward, and start twisting your upper body.

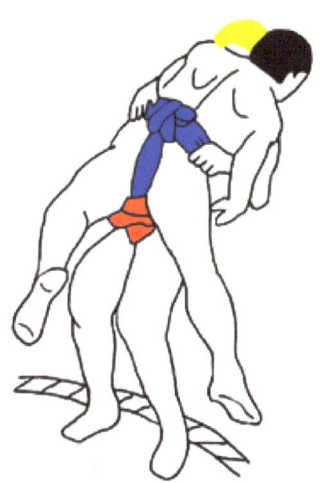

Step 2

Use your opponent's momentum and force to pull him into you and lift him off his feet.

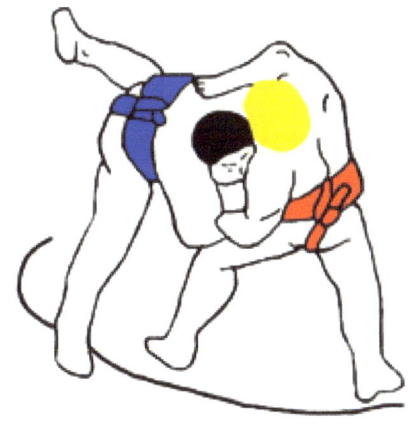

Step 3

After lifting your opponent, quickly twist your whole body and force him over and down onto his side or back.

Chapter 7

COMMONLY USED TECHNIQUES

If the last section was the meat of sumo, this section is the potatoes.

The following techniques are common methods used to win a sumo match.

Along with the frequently used, these are good techniques to learn and master.

As with any technique you will also want to learn how to defend against them because they will be used against you during the majority of your matches.

31 Common Techniques

Abisetaoshi	Leaning Force Down
Ashitori	Leg Pick
Hikkake	Arm Pull Force Out
Kainahineri	Two-Arm Twist Down
Kakenage	Thigh Hook Throw
Kekaeshi	Inside Leg Sweep
Ketaguri	Pulling Ankle Sweep
Kimetaoshi	Arm Bar Force Down
Kirikeshi	Backward Knee Trip
Komatasukui	Inside Thigh Scoop
Koshinage	Hip Throw
Kotohineri	Armlock Twist Down
Kubinage	Headlock Throw
Makiotoshi	Twist Down
Nichonage	Sweeping Hip Throw
Okurihikiotoshi	Rear Pull Down
Okurinage	Rear Throw Down
Okuritaoshi	Rear Push Down
Okuritsuridashi	Rear Lift Out
Shitatedashinage	Underarm Throw Out
Shitatehineri	Twisting Underarm Throw
Sokubiotoshi	Head Slap Down
Susoharai	Outside Leg Sweep
Susotori	Ankle Pick
Tottari	Arm Bar Throw
Tsukitaoshi	Thrust Down Backward
Uchimuso	Inner Thigh Sweep Twist Down
Ushiromatare	Backward Lean Out
Uwatehineri	Overarm Twist Down
Waridashi	Body Push Out
Watashikomi	Thigh Grab Push Down

ABISETAOSHI

Leaning Force Down

Original 70: Yes

The attacker forces his opponent over backward from a grappling position using his whole body to push opponent downward. Similar to Yoritaoshi, this technique is usually done in the ring.

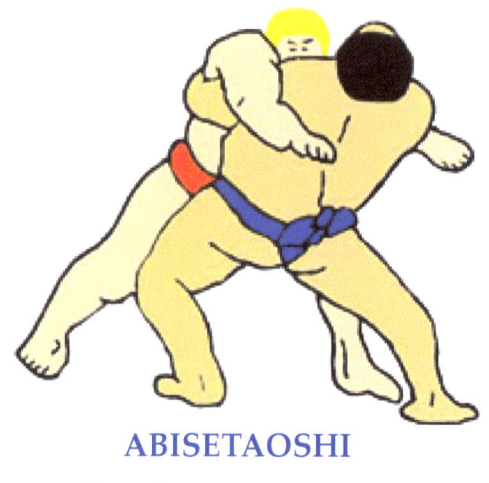

ABISETAOSHI

Leaning Force Down

Step 1

In a grappling position, force your opponent over backward by throwing your weight into him, pressuring him to lean backward.

Step 2

This technique is best used when your opponent leans backward in order to lift you up or when he is falling over backward.

When executing, release your inside grip and throw your weight onto your opponent. This technique cannot be used as an initial attack but only as a response to the situation.

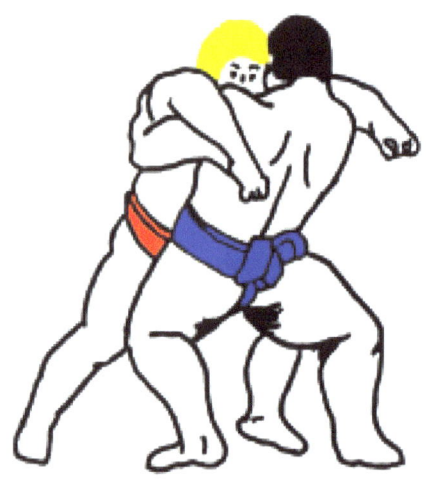

Step 3

At the final stage, lean on your opponent with all your weight. This technique is often successful when you are taller than your opponent.

ASHITORI

Leg Pick

Original 70: Yes

The attacker grabs and lifts the opponent's leg with both hands, forcing him off balance and toppling him over backward or taking him outside the dohyo. This technique is usually executed by a smaller sumotori who is gifted with quickness, agility, and the ability to complete basic sumo technique.

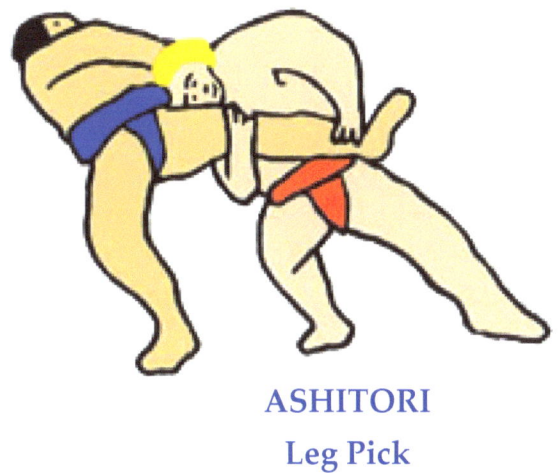

ASHITORI

Leg Pick

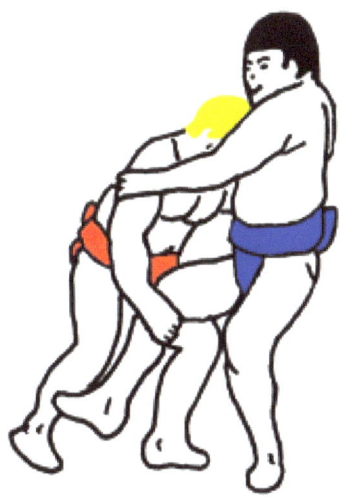

Step 1

Quickly dive under your opponent's charge, grab his thigh from the outside with one hand and behind his knee from the inside with the other hand as well.

Step 2

While lifting your opponent's leg firmly, slide your outside hand down to behind the knee or calf and your inside hand down to his ankle.

Step 3

As you grab and lift his leg, you should lean into your opponent in order to defend against his attack.

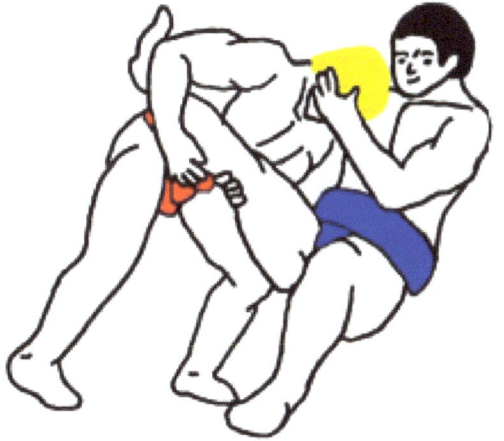

HIKKAKE

Arm Pull Force Out

Original 70: Yes

The attacker slings his opponent out of the ring by grabbing his arm with both hands—often in response to a pushing-thrusting attack—and pulling him while moving backward and to the side.

HIKKAKE

Arm Pull Force Out

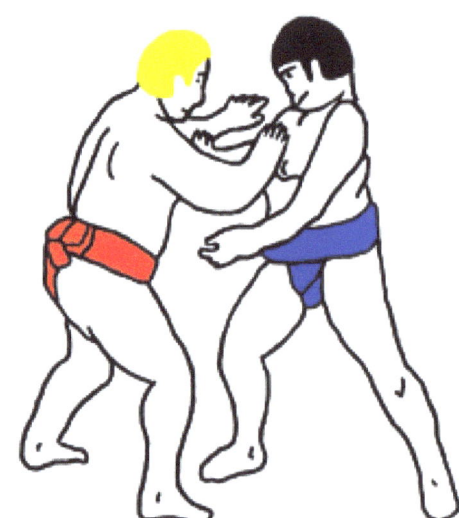

Step 1

This is best used during a heated push or thrust exchange. As a defensive move, when you are driven to the edge, shift away from your opponent's charge.

Hook or grab your opponent's arm and pull it toward you while twisting away from his charge.

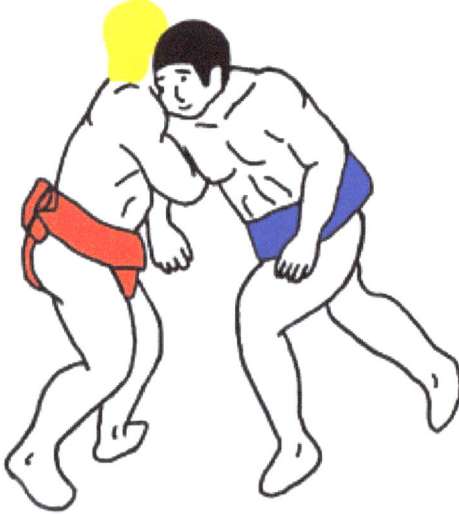

Step 2

Step 3

Grab your opponent's mawashi from behind and pull him past you and down or out of the dohyo.

KAINAHINERI

Two-Arm Twist Down

Original 70: Yes

The attacker locks up one of the defender's arms with both arms and, turning into his opponent, twists him over and into the clay.

KAINAHINERI
Two-Arm Twist Down

Step 1

Grab your opponent's right (left) arm with both your arms. This can be done with either a double outside, double inside, or one inside and one outside grip.

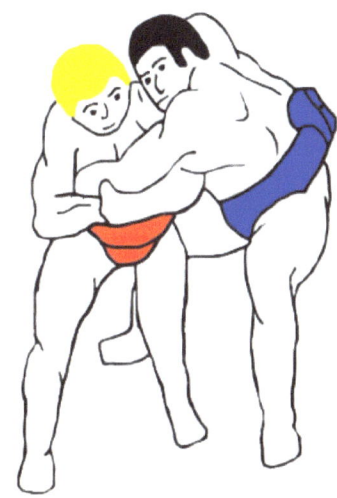

Step 2

Turn/twist away in the direction of your opponent's push with all your might. Pull your opponent over your back left (right) leg.

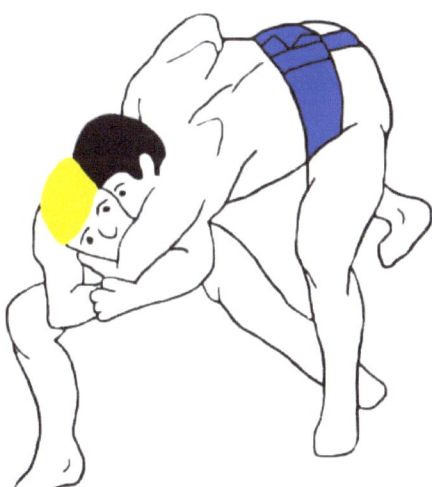

Step 3

As he is off balance, continue to pull him into you and down.

KAKENAGE

Thigh Hook Throw

Original 70: Yes

The attacker hooks one leg inside the defender's legs and turns away in order to raise the hooked leg up and back to force the defender up and over into the clay. This throw can be executed with either an outside or inside grip.

KAKENAGE

Thigh Hook Throw

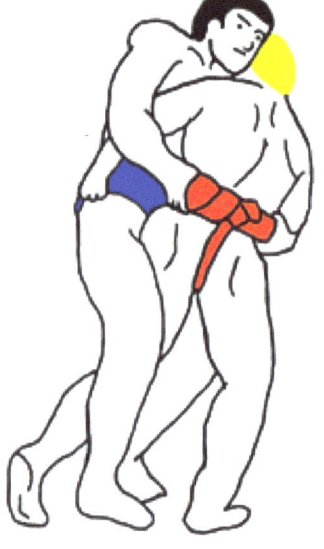

Step 1

Immobilize your opponent's arm by grabbing his forearm and pull his inside gripping hand into yourself while hooking the leg on the other side from the inside.

Step 2

Quickly lift your hooked leg to throw your opponent off balance. Swing him around in front of you and lean forward.

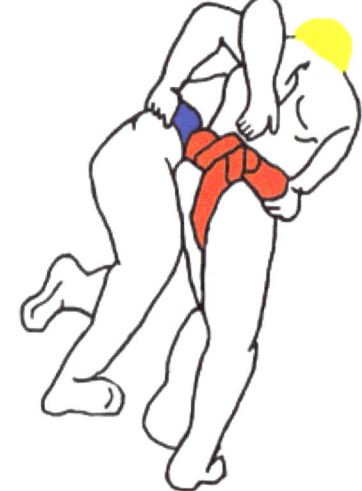

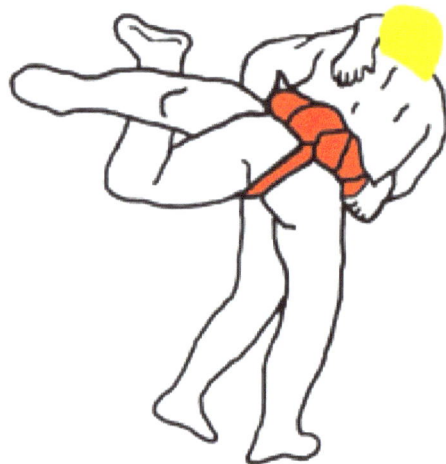

Step 3

Maintain your balance while not letting your opponent regain his and maneuver him into a position underneath you.

If you cannot successfully execute this throw on the first try, continue the throw again and again while hopping on one foot. (This is one of the throws where performing shiko correctly, by maintaining balance and low center of gravity, during keiko pays off.)

KEKAESHI

Inside Leg Sweep

Original 70: Yes

The attacker sweeps his opponent's leg out from under him by kicking the defender's leg from the inside, often accompanied by a well-timed slap on the defender's back.

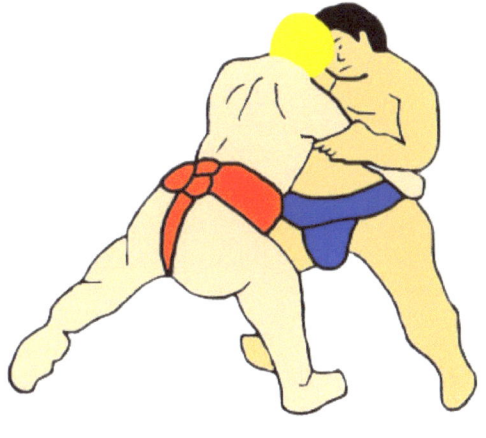

KEKAESHI

Inside Leg Sweep

Step 1

Wrap your right (left) arm around your opponent's neck and turn him into your left (right) side. At the same time, hook your right (left) leg inside his right (left) leg.

Step 2

Pull your arm wrapped around his neck and twist your right side backward.

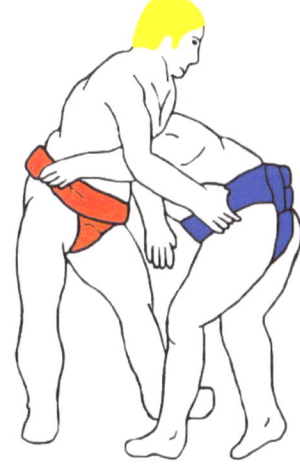

Step 3

Kick your hooked right leg forward and throw your opponent over backward.

KETAGURI

Pulling Ankle Sweep

Original 70: Yes

Usually seen at the tachiai (initial charge), the attacker leaps to the side and kicks or sweeps his opponent's lead leg from the inside while slapping the shoulder or pulling the arm closest to him. Frequently used by a fast, small sumotori to trip up a big man before he has a chance to get started.

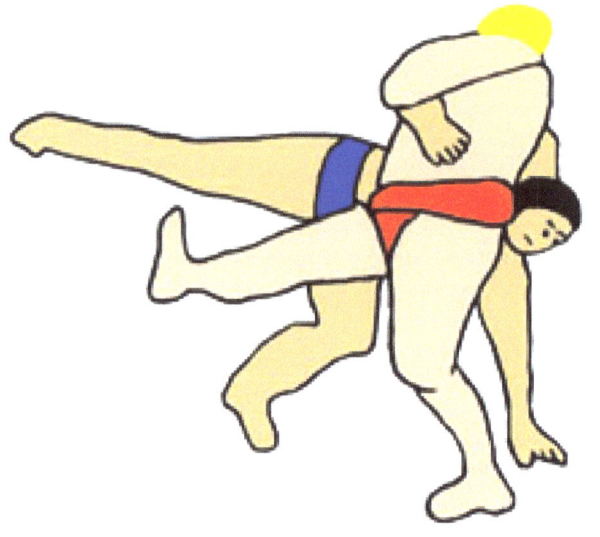

KETAGURI

Pulling Ankle Sweep

Step 1

Give the impression that you are going to make your initial change as normal.

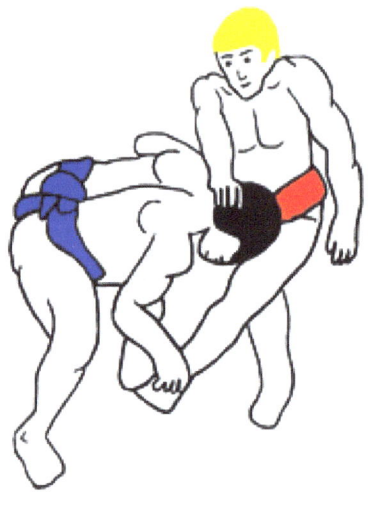

Step 2

Leap to the side and sweep your opponent's leg at the same time your opponent strikes you.

Step 3

Slap his shoulder downward or pull his arm to force your opponent to fall forward.

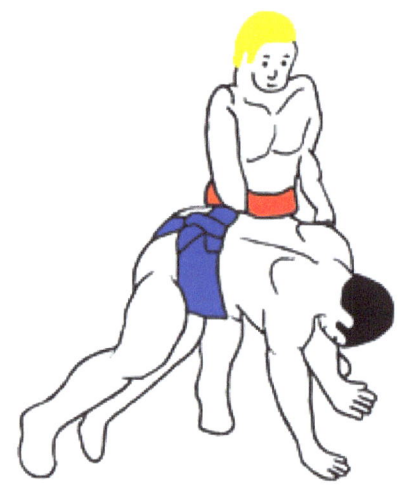

KIMETAOSHI

Arm Bar Force Down

Original 70: Yes

The attacker locks up one or both of the opponent's elbows with an outside grip, then throws his weight into and on top of the opponent.

KIMETAOSHI

Arm Bar Force Down

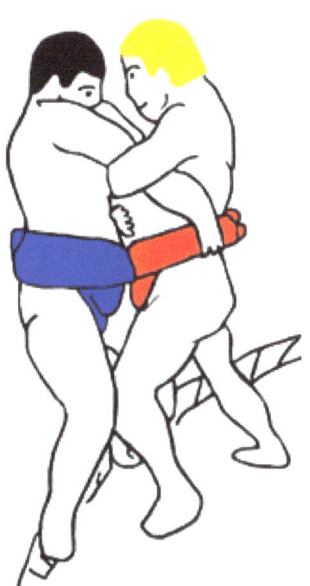

Step 1

Use this technique when your opponent has two inside grips or there is a height and strength difference between you and your opponent.

Step 2

Lock up your opponent's two inside arms with outside grips so that he cannot move. Pull up on his arms.

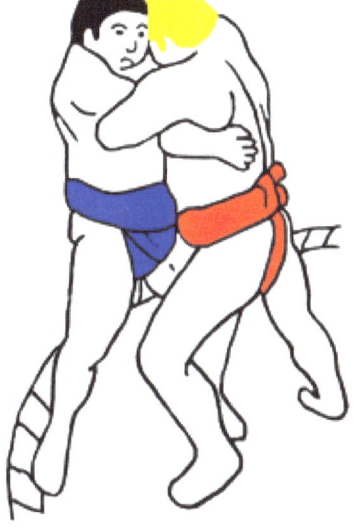

Step 3

Force your opponent back and down onto the dohyo, inside or out. Do not weaken your grip until he is down.

KIRIKAESHI

Backward Knee Trip

Original 70: Yes

The attacker takes a deep step forward, placing his knee behind his opponent's lead leg, then twists his opponent backward and over that knee. Most often used as a defensive move or counter-attack to deflect an attack and twist an opponent backward.

KIRIKAESHI

Backward Knee Trip

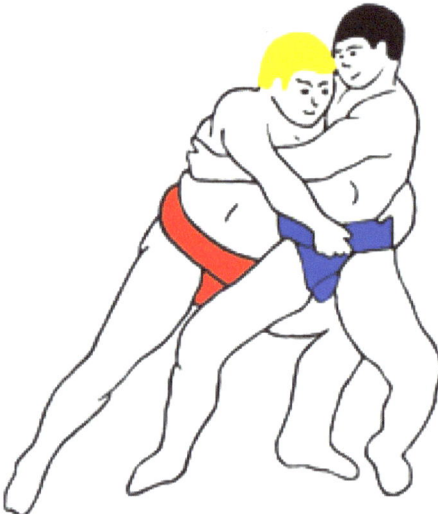

Step 1

When your opponent tries to execute a throw from the right (left) side, counter his move immediately by stepping forward with your left (right) foot to the outside/backside of his right (left) foot.

Step 2

Place your inside left (right) knee on your opponent's right (left) knee. Shift your weight (center of balance) to your left leg and attempt to bend your opponent's knee.

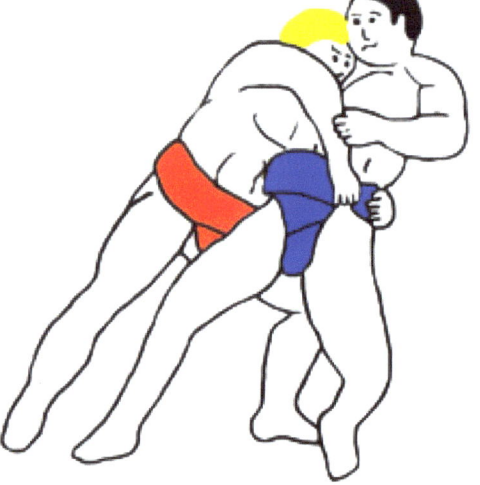

Step 3

With your right (left) arm on your opponent's chest or shoulder, push him while twisting him backward over your leg with your left (right) arm. Force him down backward by shifting your weight into your opponent.

KOMATASUKUI

Inside Thigh Scoop

Original 70: Yes

Best used in combination with an over-arm or under-arm throw. As the opponent takes a step forward to defend against the throw, the attacker grabs the opponent's leg and pulls up to drive the opponent over backward.

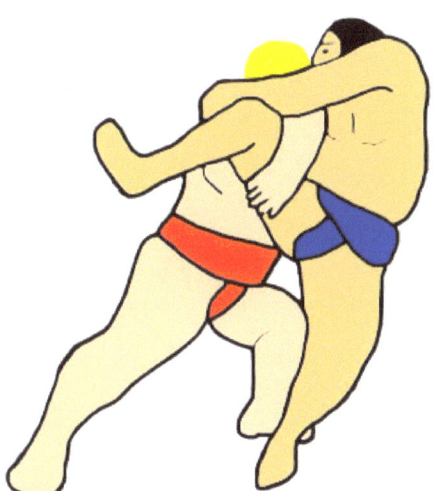

KOMATASUKUI

Inside Thigh Scoop

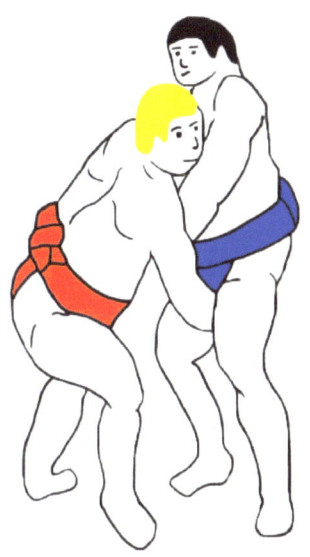

Step 1

When you are executing a throw, your opponent may defend against it by taking a step forward. If you are throwing with your left (right) arm, grab his right (left) leg, near the knee, from the inside. Very similar to omata, but in omata your opponent takes a large/long step forward.

Step 2

After grabbing the leg, pull his mawashi toward you. Drive your head and shoulder into his arm, shoulder, and chest.

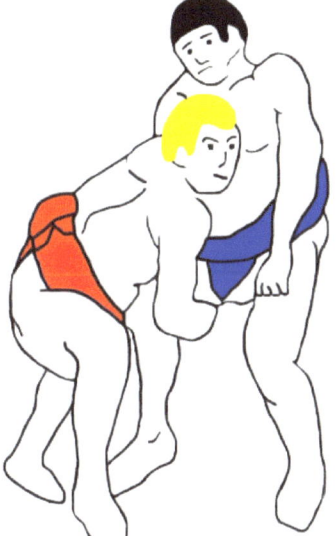

Step 3

Drive your opponent over backward by leaning into him while twisting your body and lifting his leg.

KOSHINAGE

Hip Throw

Original 70: Yes

The attacker turns into his opponent while pulling him onto his hips, straightening his knees, throwing the defender over and onto his back. This can be done with either an outside or inside grip.

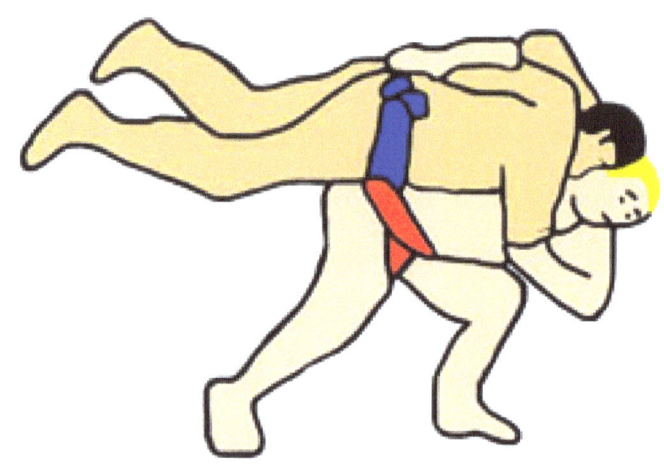

KOSHINAGE

Hip Throw

Step 1

Although this technique can be done from either an inside or outside grip, it is better used from an inside grip. It is easier for you to position your hip under your opponent from an inside grip, and it is more difficult for your opponent to defend against it.

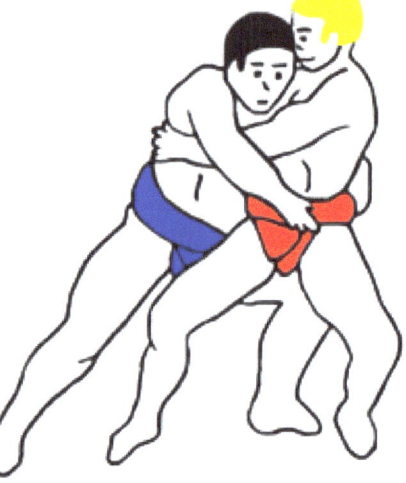

Step 2

Pull your opponent into yourself while turning him sideways. Drop your hip down and lift him up in the air using the spring action of your knees.

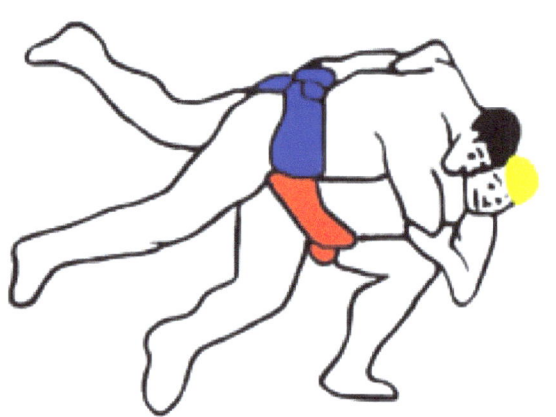

Step 3

Force your opponent to fall over while lifting him up and forward over your hip.

KOTEHINERI

Armlock Twist Down

Original 70: No

The attacker wraps his arm around the defender's inside gripping arm to lock up the defender's biceps or elbow and twists him around and down in the direction of that inside arm.

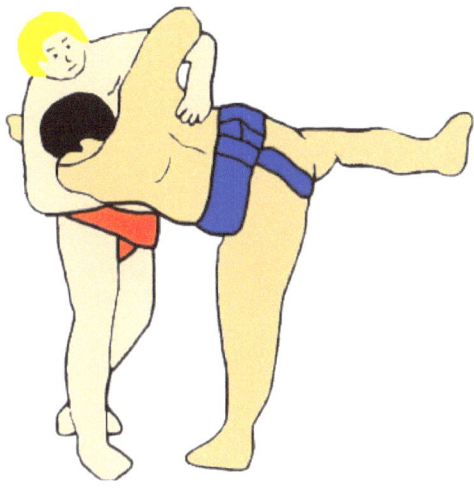

KOTEHINERI

Armlock Twist Down

Step 1

In a grappling position, use an outside arm to grab your opponent's arm.

Step 2

Lock up his bicep or elbow, rendering it useless. Your other hand can be an inside or outside grip or you may even wrap your arm around your opponent's neck.

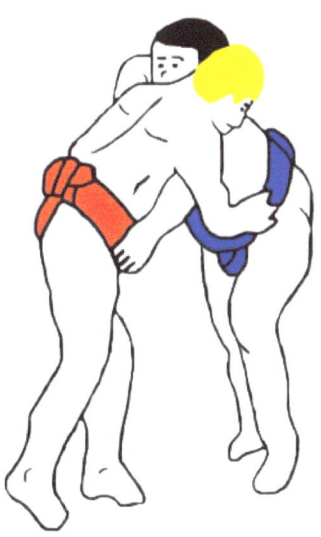

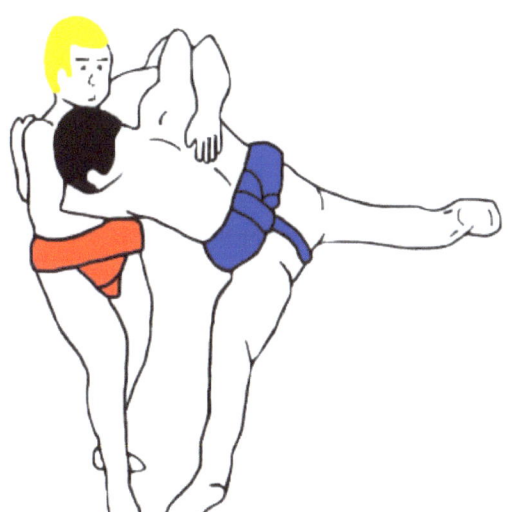

Step 3

Twist your opponent down in the direction of the wrapped arm.

KUBINAGE

Headlock Throw

Original 70: Yes

The attacker twists into his opponent and throws him by wrapping one arm around his neck as he makes that twist. The other hand is usually gripping the opponent's arm furthest from him from the outside. Usually executed as a last resort but is seldom successful.

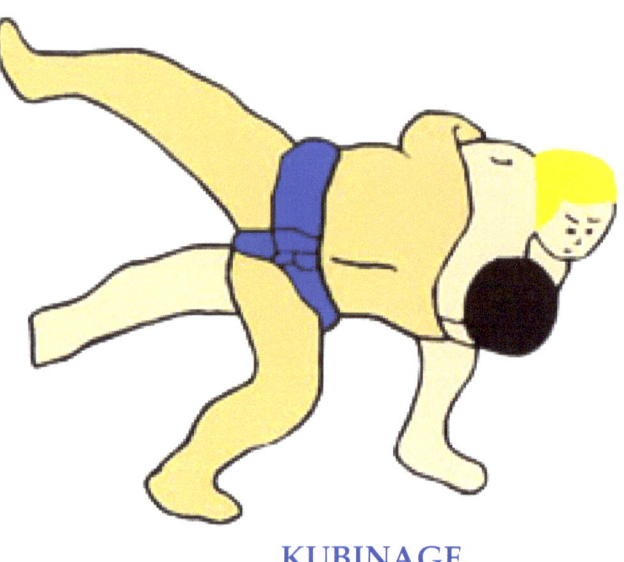

KUBINAGE
Headlock Throw

Step 1

Wrap one arm around your opponent's inside arm under his armpit and pull the arm toward you. At the same time wrap the other arm around your opponent's neck.

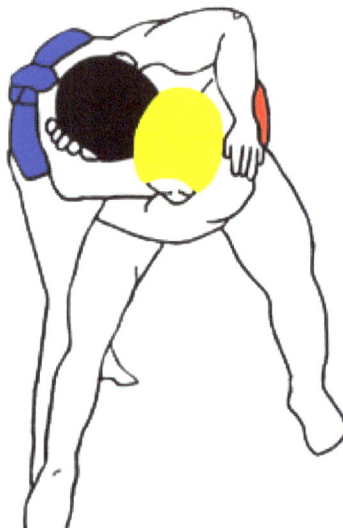

Step 2

Lean forward and throw your weight onto your opponent while twisting him in front of you.

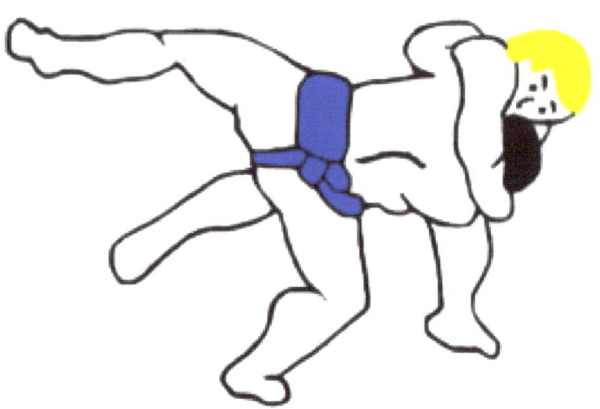

Step 3

Force your opponent onto his back on the dohyo. Your opponent's shoulders should touch first, not his hips.

MAKIOTOSHI

Twist Down

Original 70: Yes

The attacker throws his opponent by twisting him toward his own inside hand, but not gripping the mawashi.

MAKIOTOSHI

Twist Down

Step 1

When your opponent attacks by throwing his weight into you, step back with the same foot as your inside grip and turn away from your opponent.

Step 2

Turn away by taking a wide step backward and take an outside grip on your opponent with your other arm.

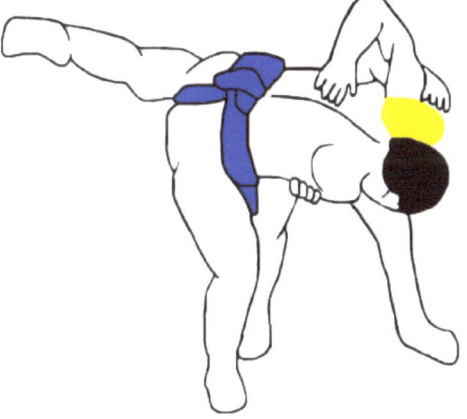

Step 3

Force your opponent to fall by continuing to twist in a downward motion.

NICHONAGE

Sweeping Hip Throw

Original 70: Yes

The attacker places one leg in front of the defender's leg, usually at the knee, then sweeps back with his leg as he pulls forward, throwing the defender over that extended leg.

NICHONAGE

Sweeping Hip Throw

Step 1

NOTE: Similar to the judo throws of haraigoshi or osotogari.

This technique is more effective when you wrap your arms around your opponent rather than taking a grip on the mawashi. Wrap your arms around your opponent and turn away from him.

Step 2

Hook your right (left) leg over your opponent's right (left) leg from the outside while continuing to twist away from him.

Step 3

Take a deep diagonal step with your opposite leg, sweep your right (left) leg back at your opponent's knee, and twist his hip over your hip/leg to cause him to become off balance and fall forward onto the dohyo.

OKURIHIKIOTOSHI

Rear Pull Down

Original 70: No

After circling behind the defender, and from any of several gripping positions, the attacker backpedals away, dropping the defender back and down.

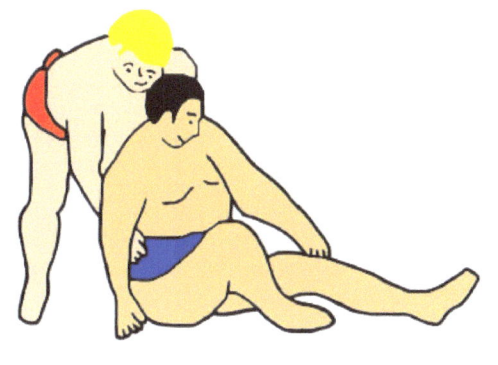

OKURIHIKIOTOSHI

Rear Pull Down

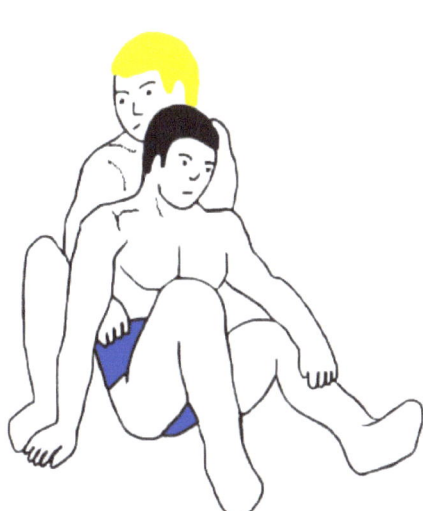

Step 1

After circling behind your opponent, pull him down toward you and force him down on his buttocks or his back.

OKURINAGE

Rear Throw Down

Original 70: No

After circling behind the defender, the attacker throws the defender forward and down, or to the side and down. To record this technique, the attacker must be standing behind the defender at the time of the throw.

OKURINAGE

Rear Throw Down

Step 1

Okuri means that the attacker is behind the defender. Very rarely will you lose if you get behind your opponent.

This technique can be done either by gripping the mawashi or not and forcing your opponent to fall by throwing him to the side or forward.

OKURITAOSHI

Rear Push Down

Original 70: Yes

Similar to okuridashi, the attacker forces his opponent down from behind to end the match before the opponent is forced over the edge.

OKURITAOSHI

Rear Push Down

Step 1

Use this technique when your opponent is pushing or thrusting you and use his power and momentum against him.

Step 2

Best used when you grab your opponent's mawashi and turn away by taking a step to the side and pulling him so that you are to his side or in back of him.

Step 3

Continue pulling/pushing your opponent from behind and force him to touch down or fall down.

OKURITSURIDASHI

Rear Lift Out

Original 70: No

After circling around the defender, the attacker drops his hips, lifts the defender up, and carries him over the edge of the ring. (* Because both of the defender's feet are in the air, the attacker can touch outside the ring with one foot before the defender's feet cross over without losing the match.)

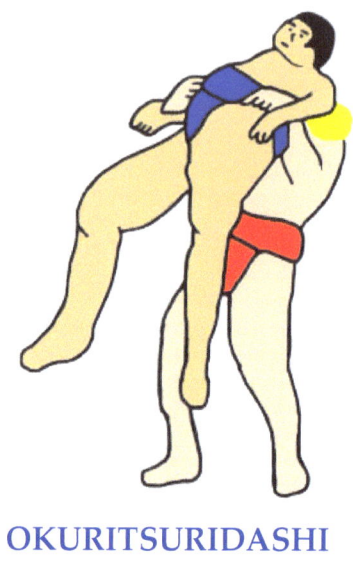

OKURITSURIDASHI
Rear Lift Out

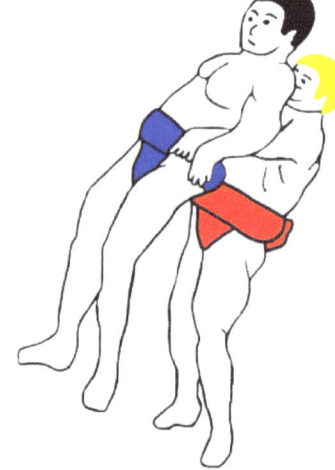

Step 1

After getting behind your opponent, lift him up into the air and carry him out of the dohyo.

Note: When performing okuritsuridashi (or similar lifting technique, e.g., tsuridashi) you are allowed to step one foot out of the dohyo and place your opponent on the ground. You must have full control of your opponent and step out forward, not sideways or backward. This is done for safety to prevent injury to either rikishi. The match is over as soon as you step out, before you place your opponent on the ground.

SHITATEDASHINAGE

Underarm Throw Out

Original 70: Yes

From an inside grip on the mawashi, the attacker turns away from his opponent, pulling him forward and down into the clay with that inside hand. Similar to shitatenage but adds a pulling motion while executing the throw.

When you pull your opponent forward and out with an inside grip, it is shitatedashinage; if you do it with an outside grip, it is uwatedashinage.

Notice when your opponent is turned a little sideways to you; this technique can be easily used.

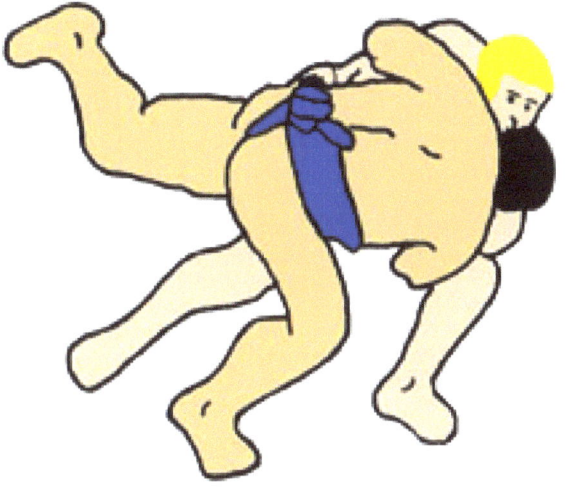

SHITATEDASHINAGE
Underarm Throw Out

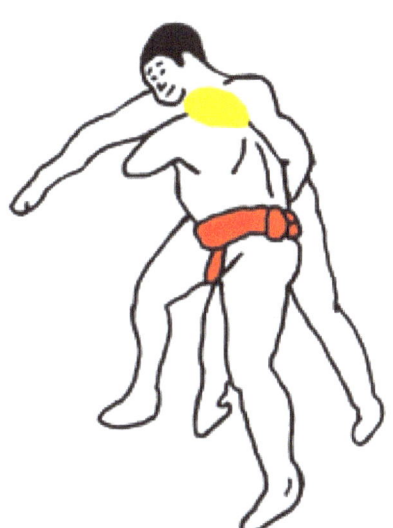

Step 1

Pull your opponent with an inside grip in the direction his knees are turned. Use your other arm to pull your opponent's head down and forward.

Step 2

It is important that you not allow your opponent to take an outside grip on your mawashi.

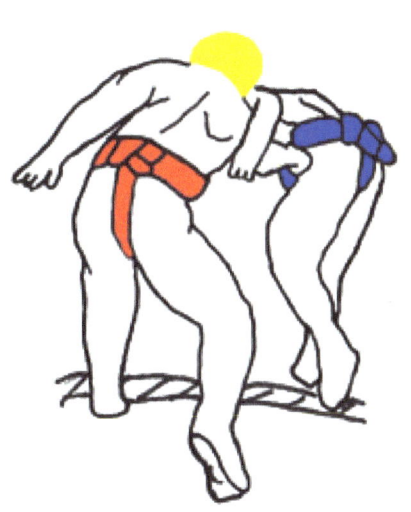

Step 3

The throw is successfully accomplished when you are centered on his body which is turned sideways.

SHITATEHINERI

Twisting Underarm Throw

Original 70: Yes

From an inside grip, the attacker twists his opponent down into the clay, pulling him in the direction of the inside hand.

SHITATEHINERI

Twisting Underarm Throw

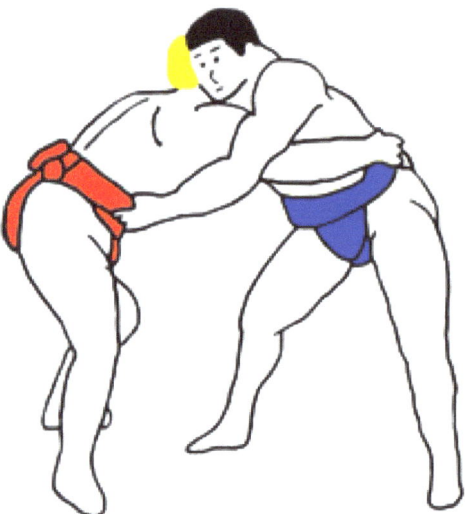

Step 1

With an inside grip of your opponent's mawashi, pull him toward you.

Step 2

As your opponent is taking a step and is off balance, quickly take a deep step backward on the same side as your inside grip and turn away.

Step 3

Continue to twist while pulling your inside grip downward to force your opponent onto the dohyo.

SOKUBIOTOSHI

Head Slap Down

Original 70: No

The attacker finds the defender leaning too far forward, then slaps down with his wrist or forearm at the defender's neck or the back of his head, forcing him to touch the ground with one or two hands.

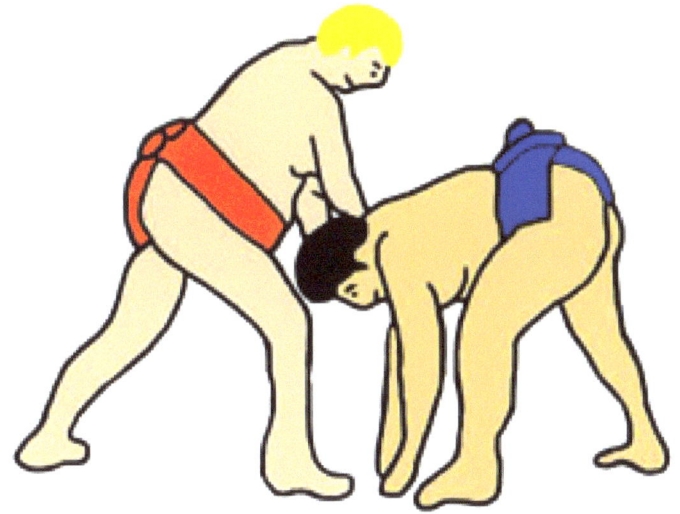

SOKUBIOTOSHI

Head Slap Down

Step 1

Best used when your opponent charges in with his head low.

Step 2

Place your hand or arm on the back of your opponent's head or neck.

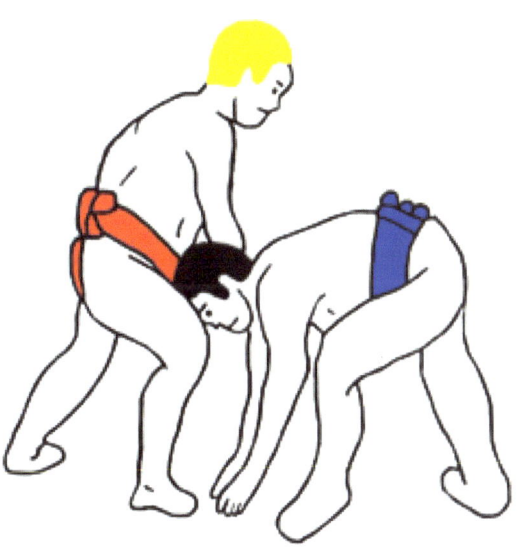

Step 3

Force your opponent to fall by slapping/pushing him down.

SUSOHARAI

Outside Leg Sweep

Original 70: Yes

The attacker uses a pulling arm throw or arm-grabbing force-out attempt to work the defender into a perpendicular position. The attacker then sweeps behind the defender's forward foot from the rear and pulls the defender backward, throwing him onto his side or back.

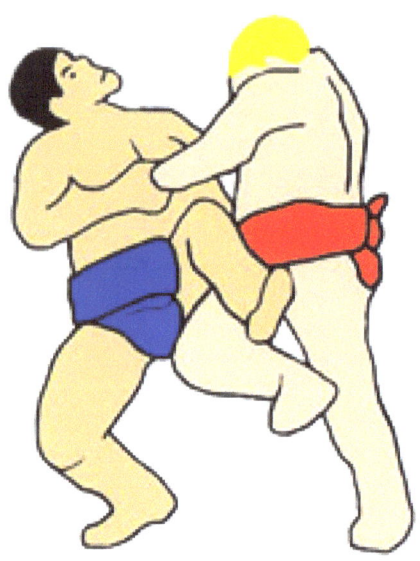

SUSOHARAI

Outside Leg Sweep

Step 1

Get on the side of your opponent by working him into a perpendicular position. This technique requires that your opponent has his weight on the leg which you attempt to sweep out from under him. Rock him back and forth.

Step 2

Sweep your opponent's ankle or heel from the rear when he takes a step forward.

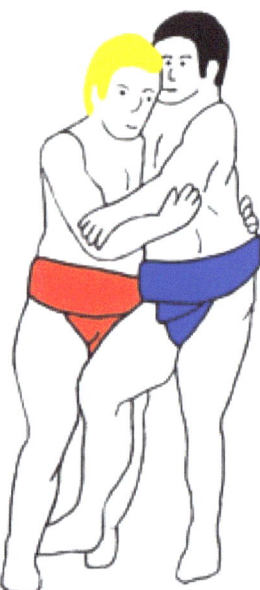

Step 3

Pull your opponent backward if you have a grip on his mawashi and/or use your free hand to push on his chest.

SUSOTORI

Ankle Pick

Original 70: Yes

As the defender attempts a throw, the attacker reaches down and grabs the ankle of his opponent's leg furthest from the defender's throwing arm. He then pulls that leg up and behind him while driving the defender over onto his back.

SUSOTORI

Ankle Pick

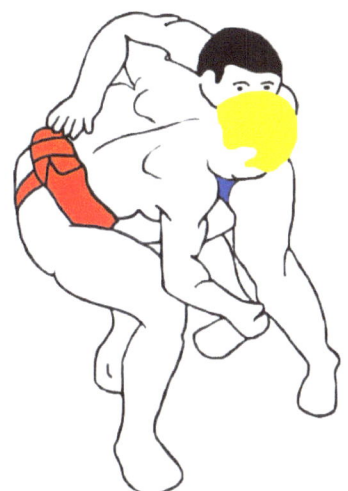

Step 1

When your opponent tries to execute a throw from the right (left) side, watch for his opposite leg to be extended in front of him.

Step 2

Quickly reach down with your right (left) hand and grab the ankle of your opponent's left leg.

Step 3

As soon as you grab your opponent's ankle, lift his leg and drive your body into him to force him over backward.

This move has to be well-timed or you will lose the match because you are so low. You also need to be careful not to touch the dohyo with your hand as you try to grab his ankle.

TOTTARI

Arm Bar Throw

Original 70: Yes

The attacker grabs one of his opponent's arms as he turns parallel to him. After wrapping his free arm around that arm from below, the attacker then bars it across his stomach or chest, forcing the opponent forward and down. Occasionally, this can be done to win by shifting away from your opponent's charge at the tachiai.

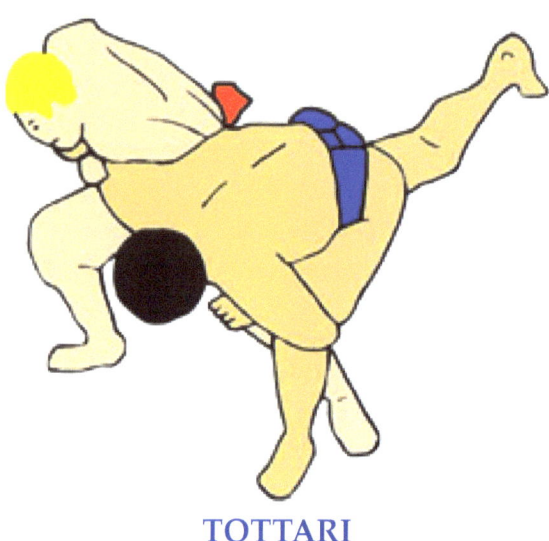

TOTTARI

Arm Bar Throw

Step 1

Grab one of your opponent's arms and turn parallel to him.

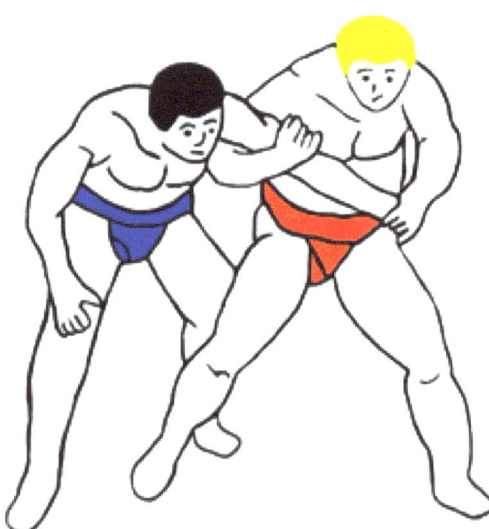

Step 2

Continue to turn away, locking up his arm, and throwing him forward and down by twisting. This requires quick action or he will get behind you and force you out.

Step 3

Force your opponent down onto the dohyo. Be sure not to lose your grip of his arm.

TSUKITAOSHI

Thrust Down Backward

Original 70: Yes

A tsuppari attack which fells the opponent, inside or outside the dohyo. After the attacker has won a heated slapping exchange, the opponent's hips are usually too far forward, and the attacker is able to thrust him over onto his back or side inside or outside the dohyo.

TSUKITAOSHI

Thrust Down Backward

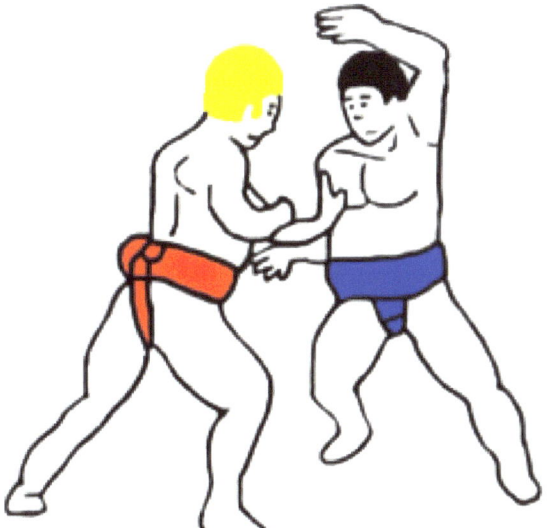

Step 1

The key to this technique is to maintain a continuous, quick rotation of thrusts from both hands. It is important to pull back on your thrusting arm quickly and slide/step forward from the same side as your thrusting arm.

Step 2

Thrust at your opponent's chest from the inside with the palm of your hand, not your fingers.

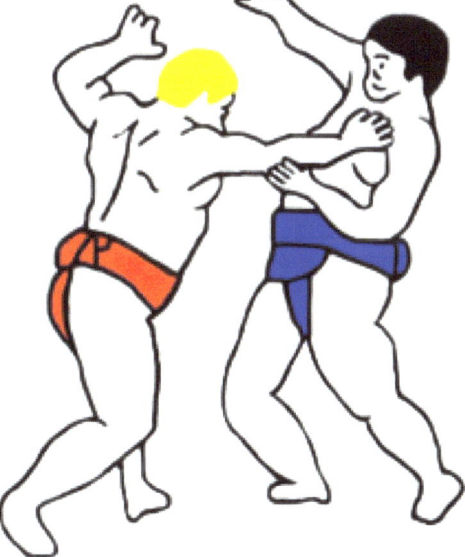

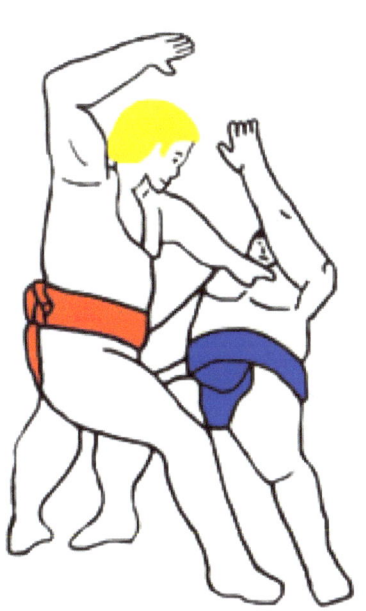

Step 3

When your opponent loses his balance and falls over backward inside or outside the dohyo because of your thrusting, your technique is called tsukitaoshi.

UCHIMUSO

Inner Thigh Sweep Twist Down

Original 70: Yes

From an inside grip, the attacker sweeps his opponent's leg up by hitting or grabbing the inner thigh with his free hand. As that hand makes contact with the opponent's thigh, the attacker pulls with his other hand in the same direction as the sweeping hand. Taking an outside grip on the leg is Sotomuso.

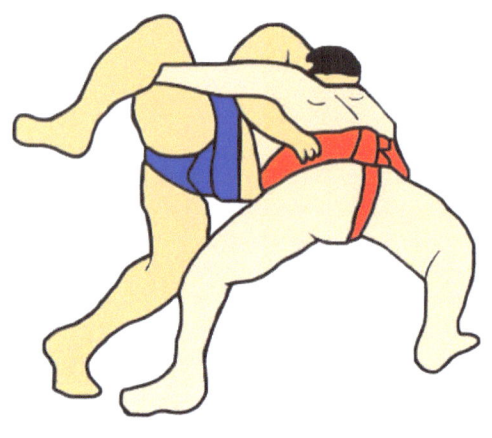

UCHIMUSO

Inner Thigh Sweep Twist Down

Step 1

When your opponent attempts to take a step, sweep his leg by hitting or grabbing the inner thigh.

Step 2

Continue to sweep his leg upward. Throw your opponent down by twisting and dropping your shoulder

Step 3

Raise the swept leg and push/pull downward with your other inside grip (usually on the mawashi, or it could be around the lower back).

USHIROMOTARE

Backward Lean Out

Original 70: No

When the defender has circled behind the attacker, usually at the edge of the ring, the attacker leans back into his opponent, forcing him back and over the edge, or back and down.

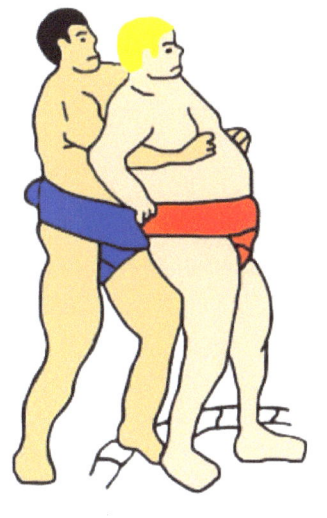

USHIROMOTARE
Backward Lean Out

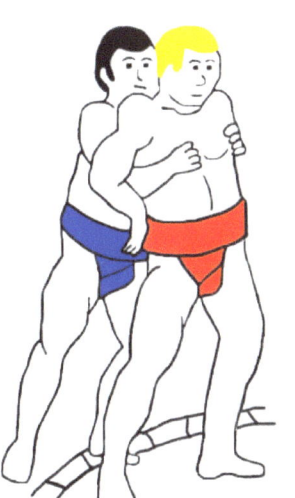

Step 1

This technique is not used intentionally, but is used as a defense when your opponent has gotten behind you, especially when he is between you and the edge of the ring.

Lean backward so that your opponent loses his balance and is forced back or over the edge of the dohyo.

UWATEHINERI

Overarm Twist Down

Original 70: Yes

From an outside grip, the attacker twists his opponent in the direction of the outside hand. This is usually seen when the opponent is defending against an overarm throw (uwantenage).

UWATEHINERI

Overarm Twist Down

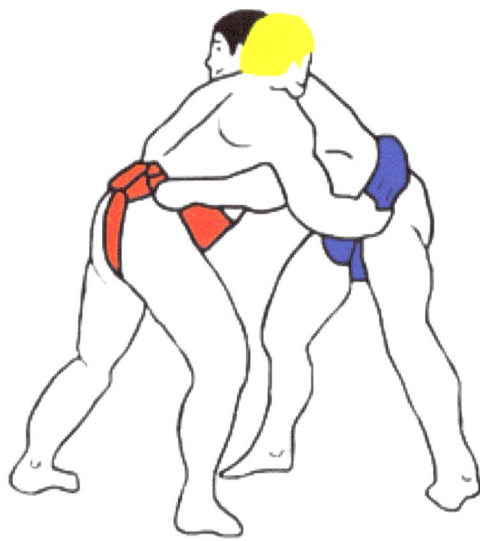

Step 1

Pull from your outside grip as in executing an overarm throw (uwatenage). As your opponent defends against the pulling by taking a step, execute this technique.

Step 2

(This throw is done in the opposite direction as uwatenage.) Take a step back with the same leg as your outside grip and twist your opponent down.

Step 3

When done successfully, your opponent will buckle his knee.

WARIDASHI

Body Push Out

Original 70: Yes

From either an inside or outside grip, the attacker grabs the defender's arm at the biceps and while pushing on that arm, drives the defender back and out. (The attacker needs significantly more strength than his opponent to execute this technique.)

WARIDASHI

Body Push Out

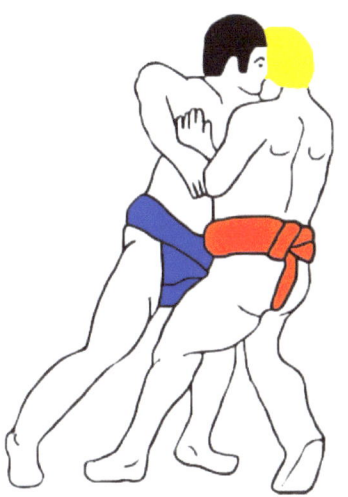

Step 1

With your hand gripping your opponent's mawashi, pull him toward you. With your other hand on his upper arm or chest, push his arms upward.

Step 2

Continue to raise the upper body of your opponent while pulling his mawashi into yourself, making him off balance.

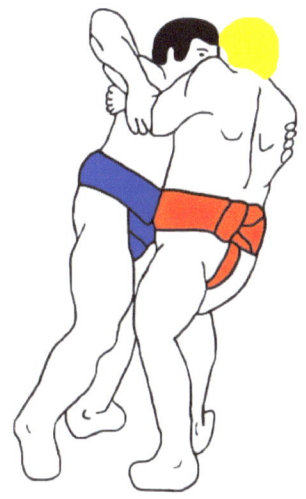

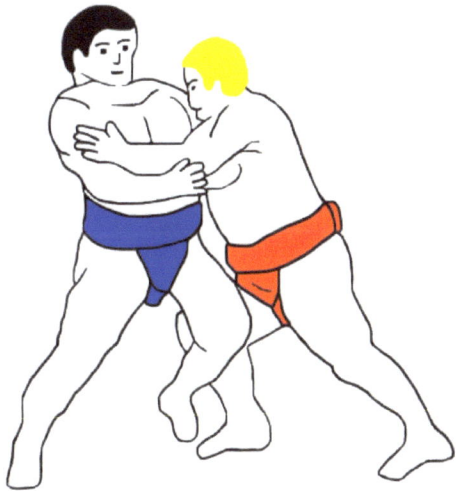

Step 3

When your opponent is standing and has a high center of gravity, extend your pushing arm forward while squatting and force your opponent back and out of the ring or down.

WATASHIKOMI

Thigh Grab Push Down

Original 70: Yes

As the attacker drives his opponent to the edge, he grabs the defender's leg at the hamstring or behind the knee. Still driving forward, the attacker pulls that leg toward him, forcing the defender either over the edge or onto his back. The attacker must lean into the defender with all his weight for successful execution.

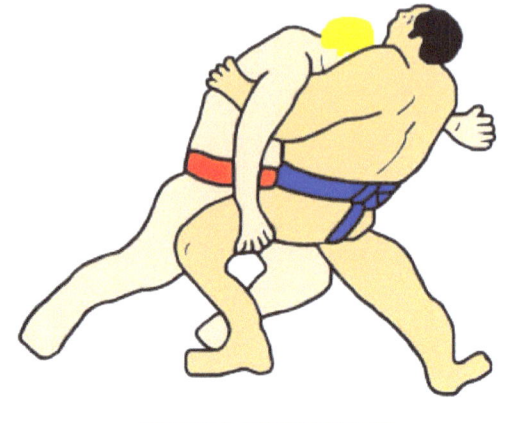

WATASHIKOMI
Thigh Grab Push Down

Step 1

When your opponent takes a step forward, grab his leg behind the knee with your outside hand.

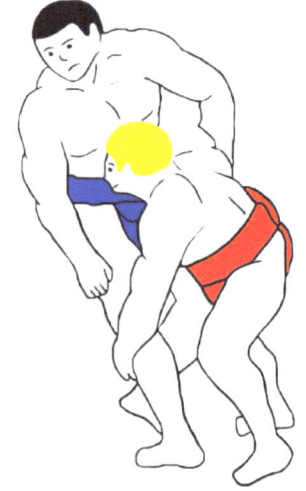

Step 2

Straighten your inside arm and push your opponent backward or push on his chest. Pull his leg toward you and upward.

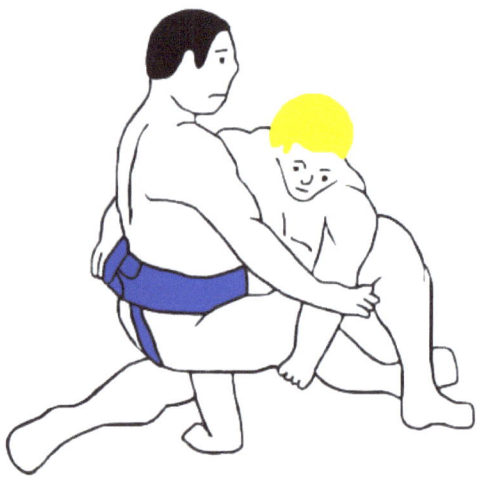

Step 3

While lifting his leg up, force your opponent over backward by leaning forward into his upper body with all your weight.

Chapter 8

UNCOMMON TECHNIQUES

These techniques are less common than the first two sections, but will be used occasionally by you and/or against you. Many of these techniques can be used when you find yourself in a precarious position and need to launch an attack or counterattack. To execute some of them, either you and/or your opponent have to be a contortionist.

As you progress further in your training, you may want to go through these techniques to develop a more rounded repertoire and to give your opponents a different look.

19 Uncommon Techniques

Amiuchi	Fisherman's Throw
Chongake	Heel Hook
Gasshohineri	Clasp-Hand Twist Down
Harimanage	Backside Belt Throw
Kawazugake	Leg Hook Reverse Throw
Kozumatori	Leg Pick
Kubihineri	Headlock Twist Down
Mitokorozeme	Triple Attack
Nimaigeri	Ankle Sweep Twist Down
Omata	Thigh Lift
Osakate	Reverse Twist Throw
Sabaori	Pulling Force Down
Sotokomata	Outside Thigh Scoop
Sotomuso	Outer Thigh Sweep Twist Down
Tsukaminage	Lift Throw
Tsuriotoshi	Lifting Body Slam
Yaguranage	Thigh Lift Throw
Yobimodoshi	Pulling Body Slam
Zubuneri	Head Pivot Throw

AMIUCHI

Fisherman's Throw

Original 70: Yes

The attacker pulls the opponent's arm with both hands in a backward twisting throw. (It resembles the traditional way of casting a Japanese fishing net.) This is normally used as an attack or defensive move to throw your opponent at the edge of the dohyo.

AMIUCHI

Fisherman's Throw

Step 1

When your opponent attempts to take an inside grip after pushing, wrap both arms around that arm and stop your opponent's attack and forward progress.

Step 2

Once you stop his momentum, be sure to use your arm on top to wrap around your opponent's inside grip arm. With your other hand/arm, grab the joint of your opponent's shoulder.

Step 3

Take a step backward with the same side leg that is holding your opponent's arm and turn away from him. Force your opponent to fall down by twisting sideways.

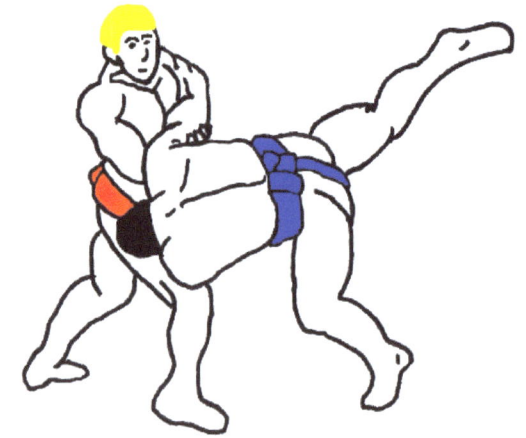

CHONGAKE

Heel Hook

Original 70: Yes

The attacker hooks his heel behind the defender's heel from the inside (left foot to left foot, or right to right) and pulls that leg toward him, grabs the defender's arm on the same side, and twists him sideways or backward into the clay.

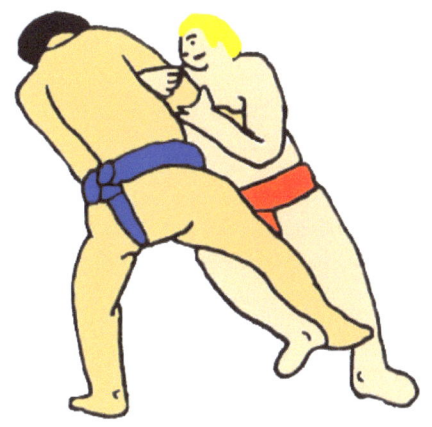

CHONGAKE
Heel Hook

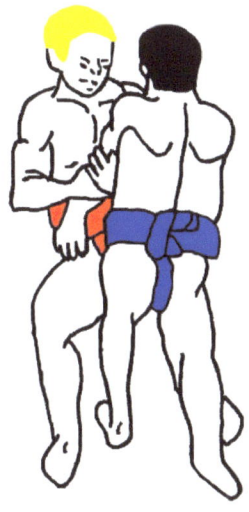

Step 1

Wrap both arms around or grab your opponent's inside arm.

Step 2

When your opponent attempts to pull his arm out of your grasp, lean forward into him and begin to hook his same leg with your opposite heel.

Step 3

As you hook his ankle with your heel from the inside, pull his leg toward you. Continue to lean into him and throw him over backward.

GASSHOHINERI

Clasp-Hand Twist Down

Original 70: Yes

Most effective with a double inside grappling grip, the attacker clasps his hands behind the defender's back and twists him down and over.

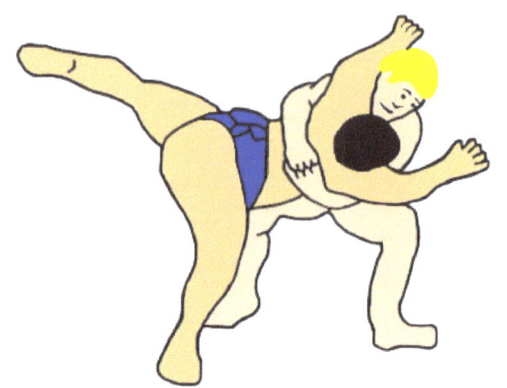

GASSHOHINERI
Clasp-Hand Twist Down

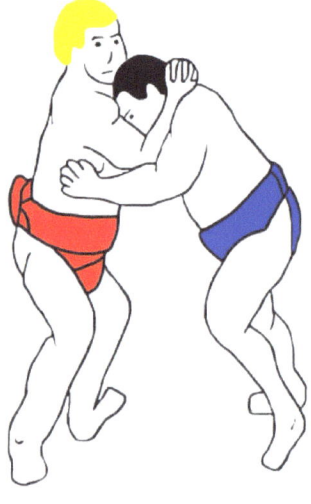

Step 1

When your opponent charges in with his head low, reach behind his head and clasp your hands together.

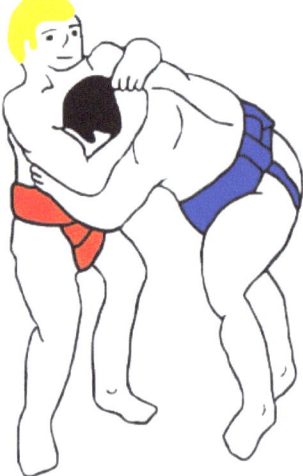

Step 2

Twist his head either to the right or left with your hands still clasped.

Step 3

Continue to twist his head in a downward motion until he falls or is out of the dohyo.

HARIMANAGE

Backside Belt Throw

Original 70: Yes

The attacker reaches over the opponent's shoulder to grab the mawashi from behind and then pulls him past his own body while twisting into him, usually as a last-ditch throw at the edge.

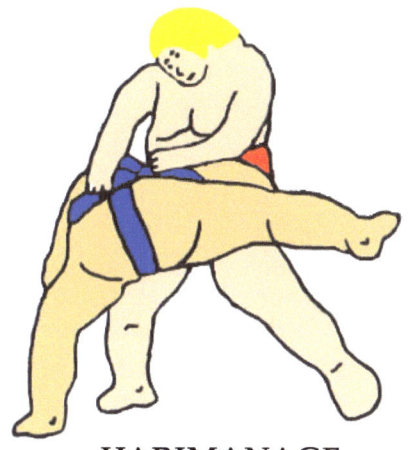

HARIMANAGE

Backside Belt Throw

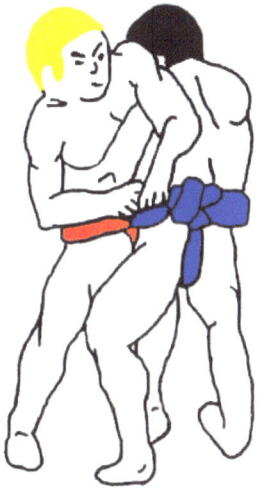

Step 1

With a right (left) hand outside grip, reach your left (right) arm over the left (right) side of your opponent's shoulder. Grab his mawashi beside your other hand's outside grip.

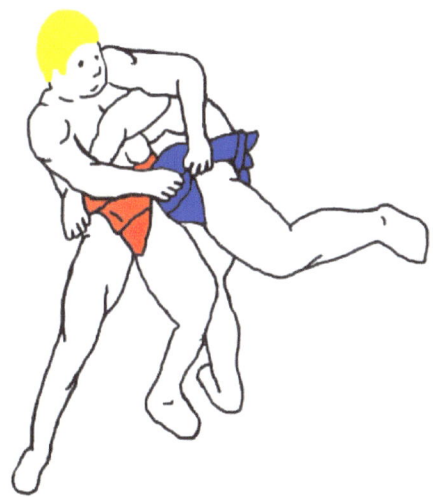

Step 2

Twist your opponent to your left (right). Pull him past yourself while leaning backward on top of him.

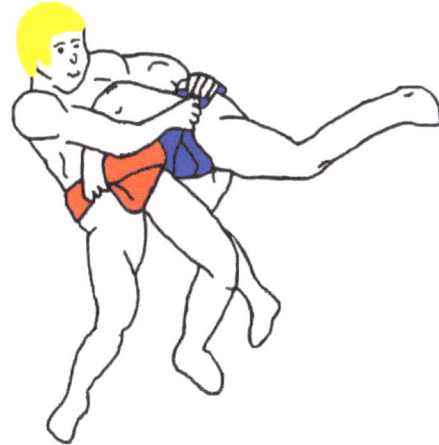

Step 3

Continue to twist and pull your opponent.

KAWAZUGAKE

Leg Hook Reverse Throw

Original 70: Yes

The attacker hooks his opponent's closest leg from the inside and takes him over backward by pulling the hooked leg forward and across his own body.

KAWAZUGAKE
Leg Hook Reverse Throw

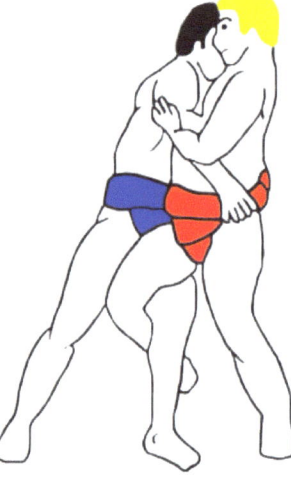

Step 1

Wrap your right (left) arm around your opponent's neck and turn him into your left (right) side. At the same time, hook your right (left) leg inside his right (left) leg.

Step 2

Pull your arm wrapped around his neck and twist your right side backward.

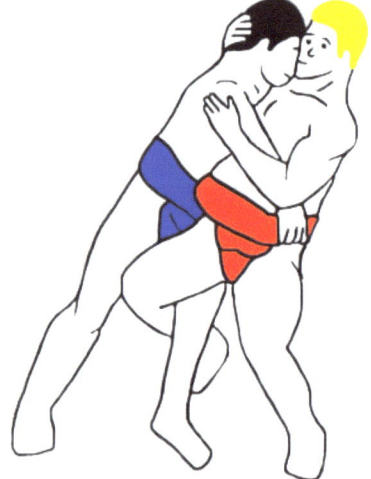

Step 3

Kick your hooked right leg forward and throw your opponent over backward.

KOZUMATORI

Leg Pick

Original 70: No

The attacker leans into his opponent and grabs the opponent's ankle or base of the calf, then pulls that ankle up and toward him while driving into his foe, forcing him over onto his back. Another variation has the attacker pulling on the same ankle or calf from behind.

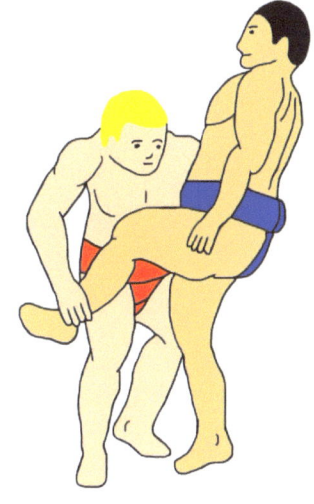

KOZUMATORI

Leg Pick

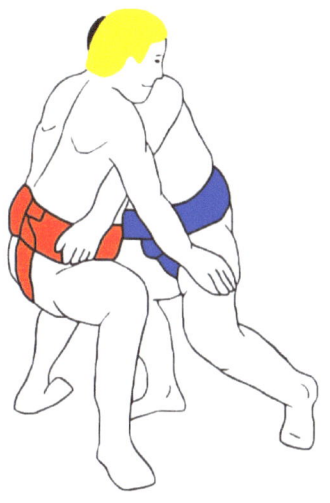

Step 1

From a grappling position, you cause your opponent to lose balance by executing a throw.

Step 2

While your opponent's leg is in the air, grab his ankle or base of his calf.

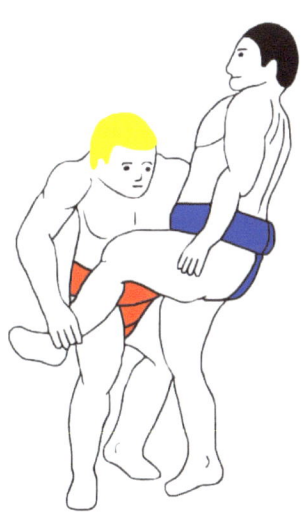

Step 3

Pull the ankle up and force your opponent over onto his back.

KUBIHINERI

Headlock Twist Down

Original 70: Yes

The attacker wraps one hand around his opponent's neck and the other hand around the opponent's inside gripping arm, then pulling the hand on the opponent's neck and twisting the opponent onto the clay.

KUBIHINERI

Headlock Twist Down

Step 1

When your opponent attempts to take an inside grip, grab or hold that arm and pull it into you while your other arm is wrapped around his neck.

Step 2

Twist the wrapped arm side downward.

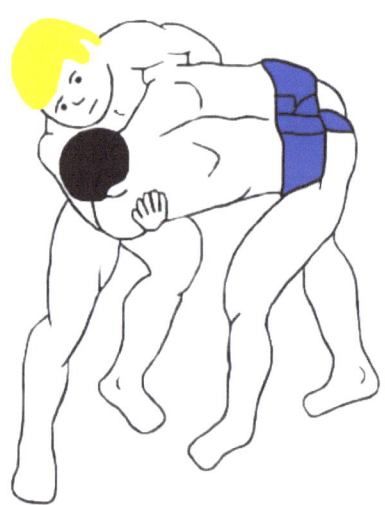

Step 3

Throw your opponent down by twisting his neck/shoulders while continuing to twist his wrapped arm downward.

MITOKOROZEME

Triple Attack

Original 70: Yes

Executing three techniques almost simultaneously, the attacker attempts an inside leg trip with one leg, grabs the defender's other leg behind the thigh and tries to pull that leg out from under him, and drives his head into his opponent's stomach or chest to force him backward.

MITOKOROZEME

Triple Attack

Step 1

Hook your leg inside your opponent's leg while burying your head into his chest.

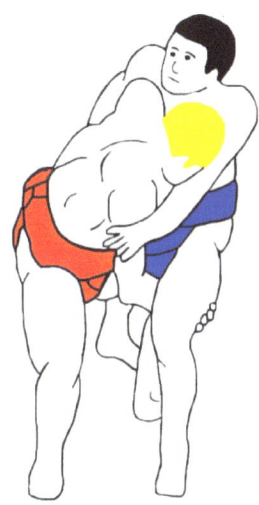

Step 2

Grab your opponent's other leg and lift it up.

Step 3

Continue to drive your head and shoulders into your opponent's chest while pushing him over backward.

NIMAIGERI

Ankle Sweep Twist Down

Original 70: Yes

The attacker pulls his opponent into him and kicks the defender's legs out from under him by striking the outside of the defender's ankle with the sole of his foot, sweeping left to right or right to left. The attacker then uses his upper body to throw or twist the defender onto his side or back.

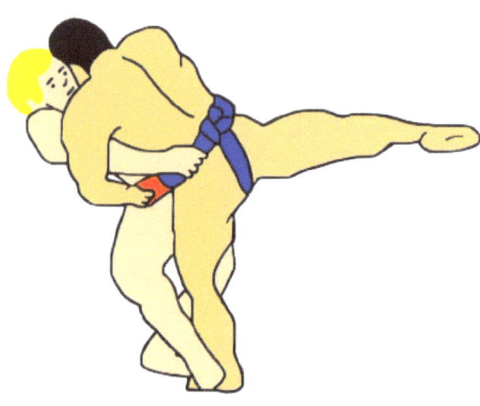

NIMAIGERI
Ankle Sweep Twist Down

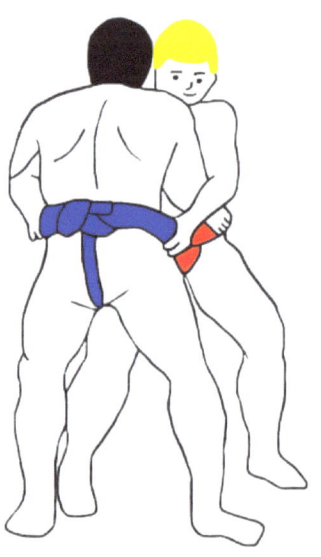

Step 1

Pull your opponent into you with both hands on his mawashi. Lift your opponent as much as possible. Make a special effort on your outer hand as it is more effective to kick out your opponent's leg from the same side as your inside grip.

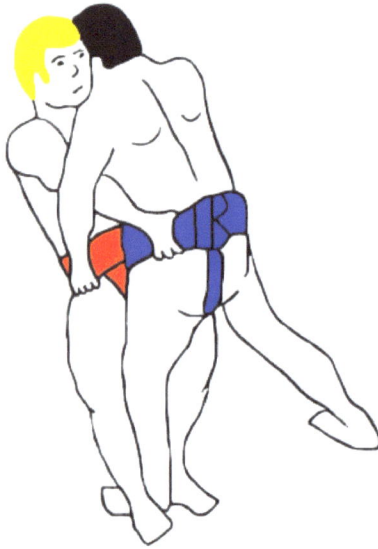

Step 2

Fully inflate your chest to draw your opponent as close as possible. Sweep your opponent's leg that is on your inside grip side.

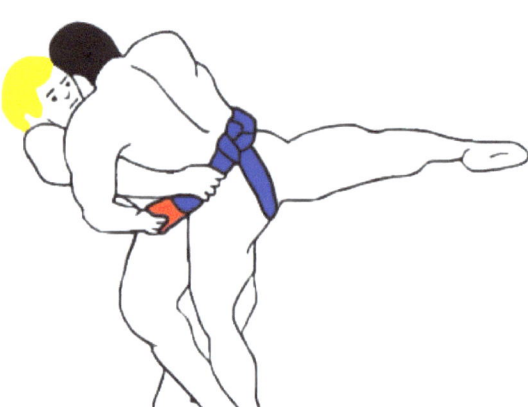

Step 3

Use your upper body to throw or twist him onto the dohyo.

OMATA

Thigh Lift

Original 70: Yes

When the defender attempts to block an overarm or underarm throw by taking a deep step forward, the attacker grabs that leg from the inside with his free hand and lifts it up and backward, driving his body into the defender and forcing him over onto his back.

OMATA
Thigh Lift

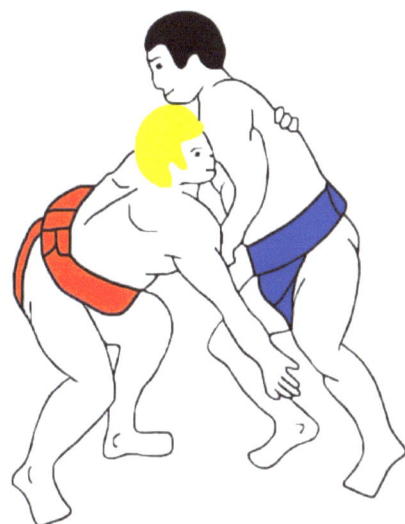

Step 1

Omata means "long stride or step." The difference between omata and komatasukui is that in omata your opponent takes a step forward in defense against a throw. You then grab that leg with an inside grip at his knee or lower thigh.

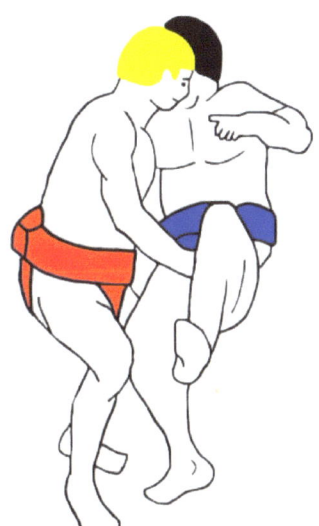

Step 2

Lift your opponent's leg as high as possible.

Step 3

Lean into your opponent while continuing to lift his leg and force him over backward or to the side.

OSAKATE

Reverse Twist Throw

Original 70: No

From a deep, standard outside grip, usually at the edge of the ring, the attacker bends backward and swings his opponent around and out in the direction of that outside gripping hand. Best used when your opponent charges in with his head low.

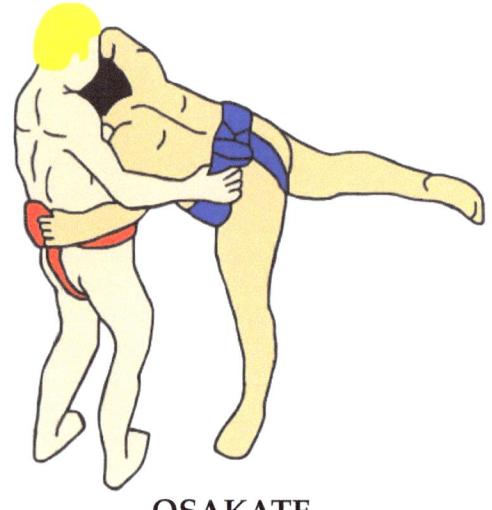

OSAKATE
Reverse Twist Throw

Step 1

This technique is best used when your opponent charges in with his head and shoulders low.

Step 2

Reach over your opponent's shoulder and take a deep outside grip on his mawashi.

Step 3

Throw your opponent with your outside grip on the mawashi. If you are on the tawara, you may have to twist; otherwise you may be able to step back with your opposite foot while twisting.

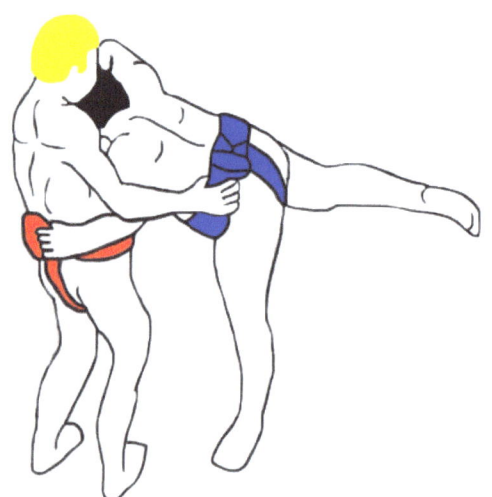

UNCOMMON

SABAORI

Pulling Force Down

Original 70: Yes

With both hands on his opponent's mawashi, the attacker pulls the defender in, throwing his weight high into and on top of the defender, causing the defender's knees to buckle.

SABAORI

Pulling Force Down

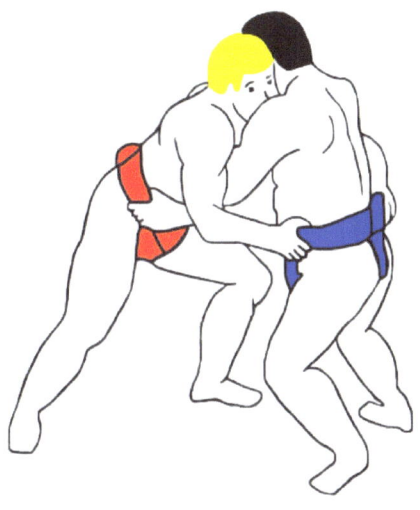

Step 1

If your opponent has a double inside grip, drive your upper body into him taking a double outside grip on his mawashi.

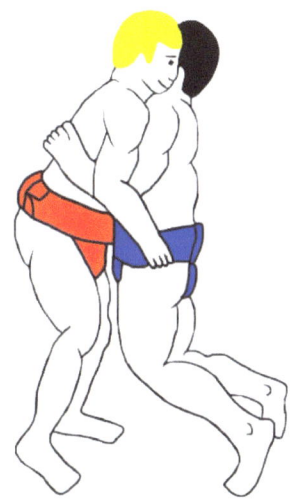

Step 2

When your opponent tries to force you out by leaning into you with his upper body, force him down by placing your jaw on his shoulder, use your upper body to get him to lean backward.

Step 3

With a double grip on your opponent's mawashi, pull/push his hips downward to the dohyo.

SOTOKOMATA

Outside Thigh Scoop

Original 70: Yes

As the defender steps forward, the attacker grabs the lead leg from the outside, then lifts the leg, driving his opponent over backward.

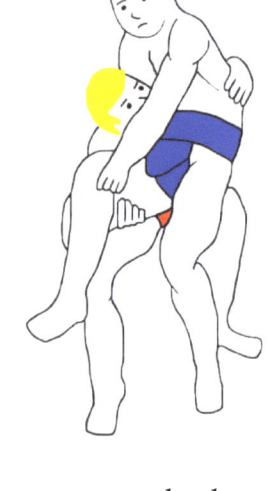

SOTOKOMATA

Outside Thigh Scoop

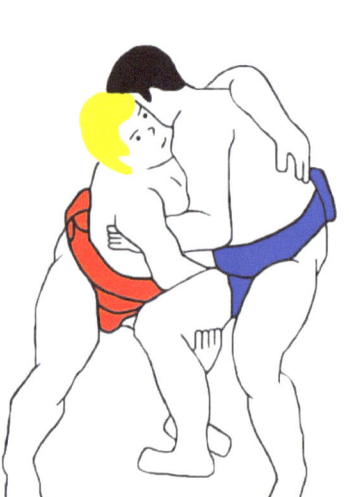

Step 1

As your opponent defends against your throw by stepping forward, immediately get to the side of your opponent and grab his leg near the knee from the outside.

Step 2

Squat and lift your opponent's leg as high as possible.

Step 3

While lifting your opponent's leg, drive your upper body into him and force him over backward.

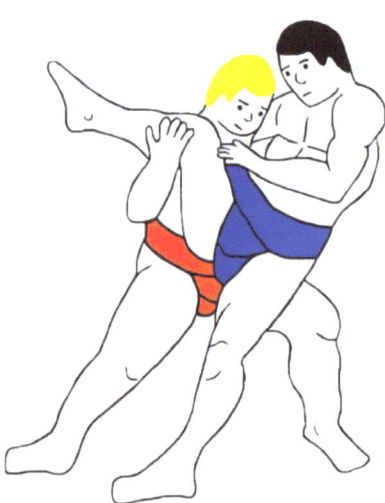

SOTOMUSO

Outer Thigh Sweep Twist Down

Original 70: Yes

The attacker releases his inside gripping hand and reaches across the front of the defender's body to block or prop the defender's far leg. At the same time, he locks up the defender's inside-gripping arm while twisting his body into his opponent. With the defender's far leg blocked from stepping forward, this forces him to fall over onto his back.

SOTOMUSO

Outer Thigh Sweep Twist Down

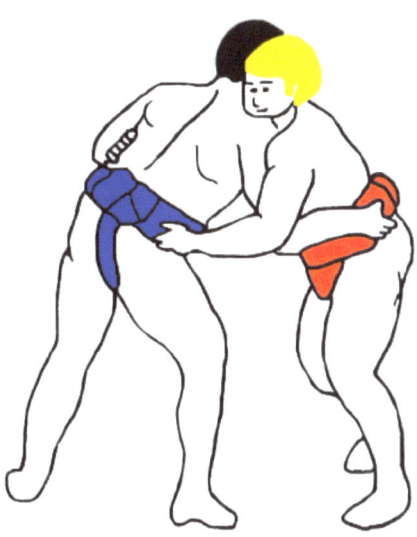

Step 1

With one inside and one outside grip, drive your opponent backward. As he defends with a counter drive, grab his inside arm at or above the elbow.

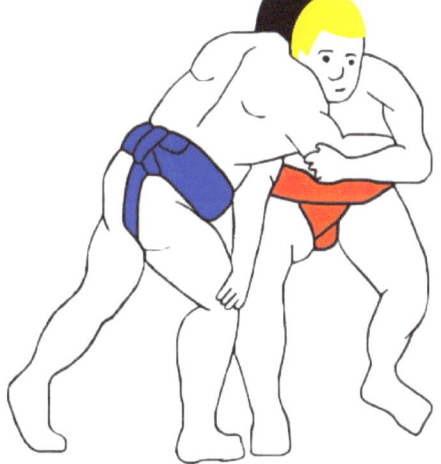

Step 2

Release your inside grip and grab your opponent's knee from the outside.

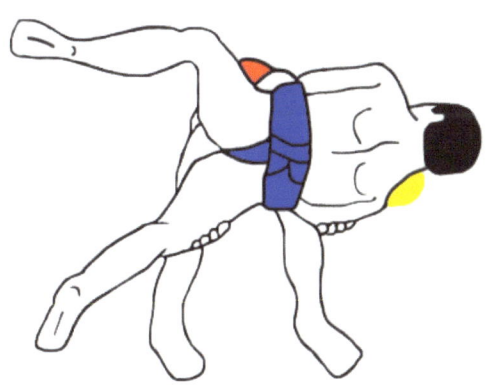

Step 3

Continue twisting your body in a downward motion so that your opponent falls over backward.

TSUKAMINAGE

Lift Throw

Original 70: Yes

From an outside grip, the attacker pulls his opponent past him. As he completes the pull, he will heave the defender into the air and then drive him into the clay. The motion of this technique is always right to right or left to left. Tsukami means to "grip, clamp, or shackle"

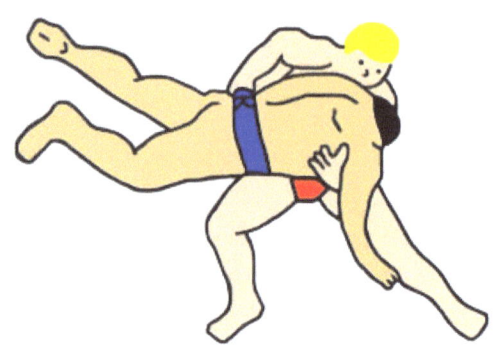

TSUKAMINAGE
Lift Throw

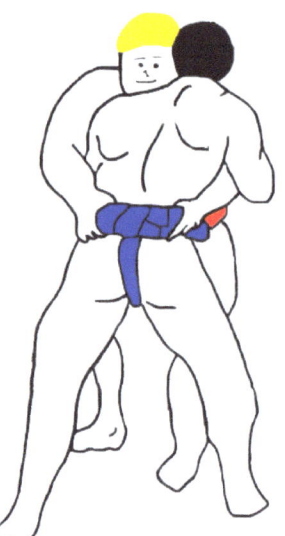

Step 1

When your opponent attempts to take a deep inside grip, step back a little with the same foot of his inside grip.

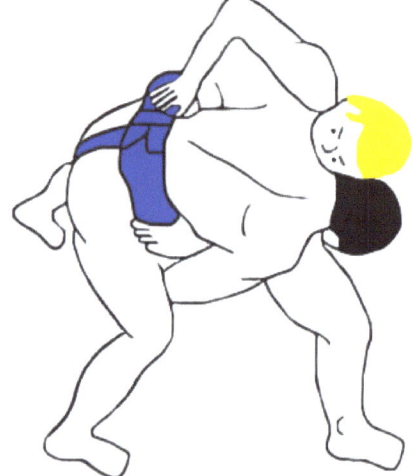

Step 2

Twist your hips and take an outside grip on your opponent's mawashi from behind.

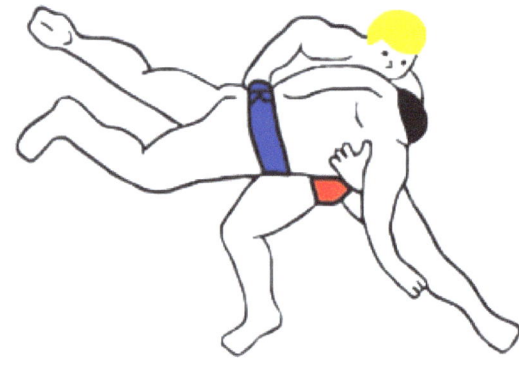

Step 3

Continue to twist your hip and use it to lift your opponent into the air. Throw your opponent down onto the dohyo.

UNCOMMON

TSURIOTOSHI

Lifting Body Slam

Original 70: Yes

In this power technique, the attacker drops his hips while pulling the defender in, then lifts him into the air. But rather than deposit his opponent outside the ring, the attacker swings his opponent sideways and drives him into the clay. Used when the opponent's struggling prevents lifting him out of the dohyo.

TSURIOTOSHI
Lifting Body Slam

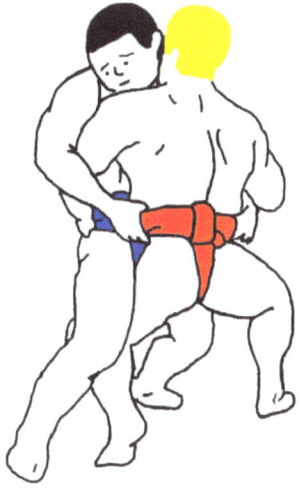

Step 1

Pull your opponent toward you and lower your hips so that your mawashi is lower than your opponent's.

Step 2

Lift your opponent into the air. Do not let him create space between your upper bodies. Pull/keep his mawashi in tight to yours.

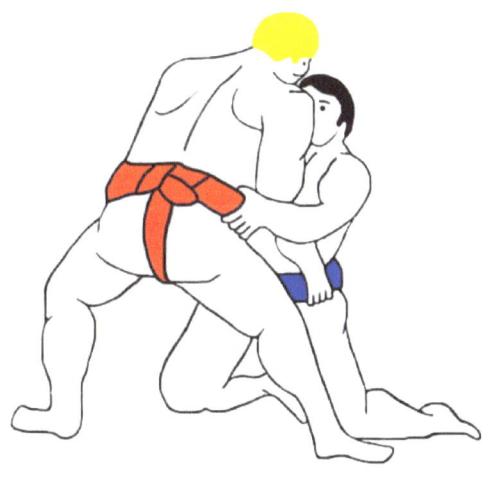

Step 3

Swing your opponent sideways and drive him down into the clay.

UNCOMMON

YAGURANAGE

Thigh Lift Throw

Original 70: Yes

From either an inside or outside grip, the attacker pulls his opponent into him, drops his hips, and places the outside of his knee against the defender's inner thigh. From here, he starts the throwing motion, driving that leg up, forcing the defender over onto his side.

Yagura is a tower/turret. It is also where the drum for announcing a sumo tournament is played. This term is derived from both rikishi standing upright/tall and close together while the kimarete is being executed.

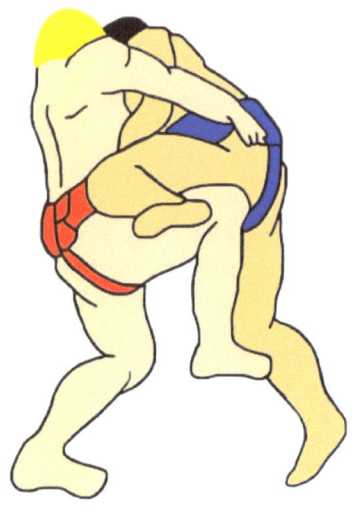

YAGURANAGE
Thigh Lift Throw

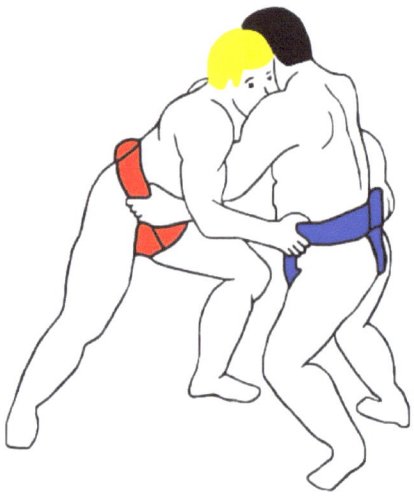

Step 1
Take a double grip and pull your opponent toward yourself.

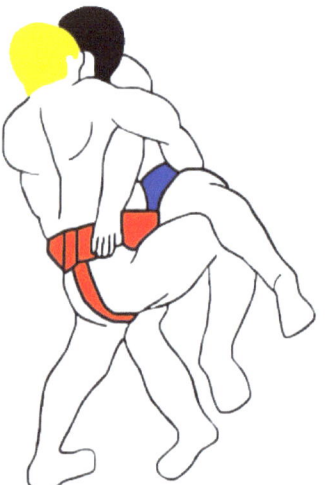

Step 2
Place your knee against your opponent's inner thigh and raise your leg.

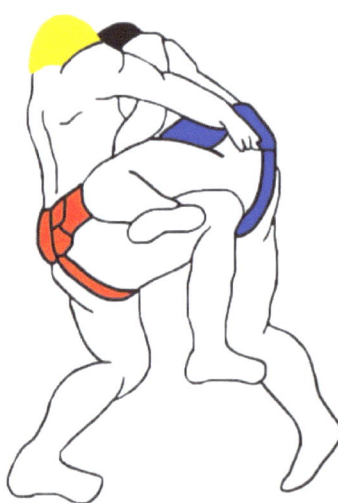

Step 3
After lifting your opponent's leg and disrupting his balance, swing him to the side and onto the dohyo.

YOBIMODOSHI

Pulling Body Slam

Original 70: Yes

This power technique is seen only when there is a wide gap in strength between the two opponents. The attacker pulls the defender in the direction of the attacker's inside grip. Then, using the defender's reaction against that pull, he releases his inside grip, turns his palm down, and takes the defender in the other direction, heaving him off his feet.

YOBIMODOSHI

Pulling Body Slam

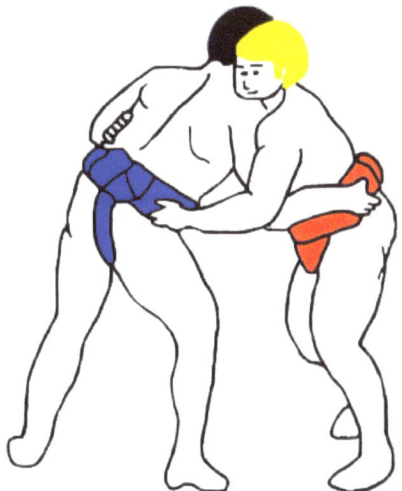

Step 1

Pull your opponent into you with your inside grip.

Step 2

As your opponent reacts against the pull, use his reaction and very quickly release your inside grip, turn your palm outward, and extend your arm upward, lifting your opponent's arm with your upper arm/elbow. (This is a move that you perform during one variation of suriashi and is used at other times to keep your opponent off your mawashi.)

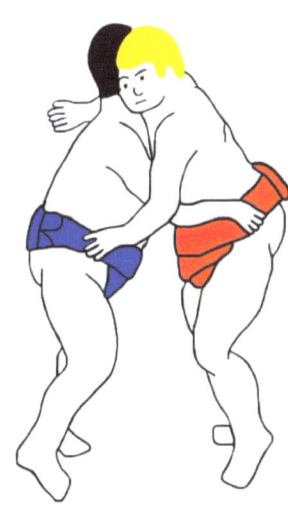

Step 3

Your opponent will have a high center of gravity; twist him down in the direction of your outside grip and force him down onto the dohyo.

ZUBUNERI

Head Pivot Throw

Original 70: Yes

The attacker buries his head in the defender's chest and then locks up the defender's inside arm by wrapping his own arm around it. He then twists that inside arm across his own body and uses his head as a fulcrum to spin the defender around and over onto his back.

ZUBUNERI
Head Pivot Throw

Step 1

Place your head near your opponent's shoulder during a heated push exchange. Do not grip his mawashi.

Step 2

Wrap your outside arm around your opponent's inside arm and lock it up at the elbow.

Step 3

Once your opponent raises his foot (opposite of your grip on his arm) step back and twist (same side as your grip). Use your head as a fulcrum and continue to twist as you grab his other arm to swing him around and down onto the dohyo.

Chapter 9

RARE TECHNIQUES

These techniques are not seen very often. Some are difficult to perform; others require unique positioning; and some require a great deal of strength and/or quickness. A few can be dangerous to execute, and you should use caution when trying to perform them.

They are included as part of the 82 winning techniques officially recognized by the Japan Sumo Kyokai.

12 Rare Techniques

Ipponzeoi	One-Arm Shoulder Throw
Izori	Backward Body Drop
Kakezori	Leg Hook Backward Body Drop
Okurigake	Rear Leg Trip
Okuritsuriotoshi	Rear Lift Body Slam
Sakatottari	Arm Bar Throw Counter
Shumokuzori	Bell Hammer Backward Body Drop
Sototasukizori	Outside Reverse Backward Body Drop
Tasukizori	Inside Reverse Backward Body Drop
Tokkurinage	Two-Hand Head Twist Down
Tsumatori	Rear Leg Pick
Tsutaezori	Underarm Forward Body Drop

IPPONZEOI

One-Arm Shoulder Throw

Original 70: Yes

Similar to the judo technique of the same name, the attacker heaves his opponent over his shoulder or hip.

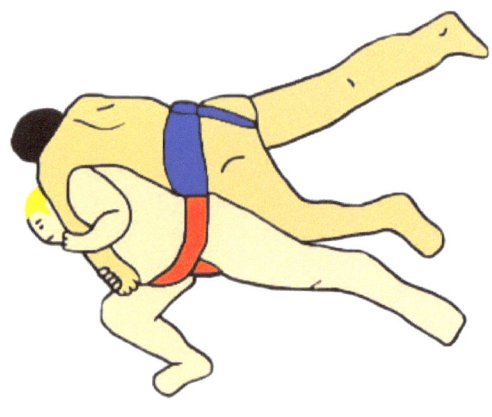

IPPONZEOI

One-Arm Shoulder Throw

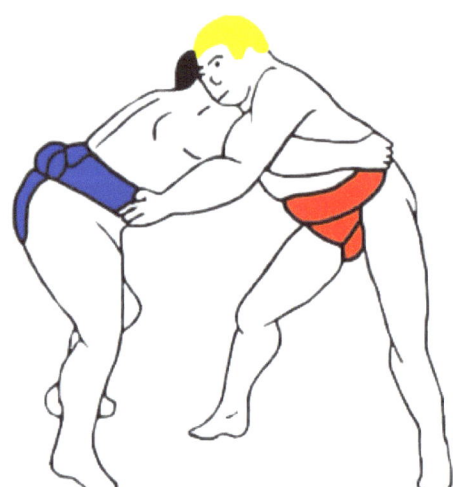

Step 1

After attacking, when your opponent charges forward or starts a thrusting attack, grab your opponent's wrist immediately and get it over your shoulder.

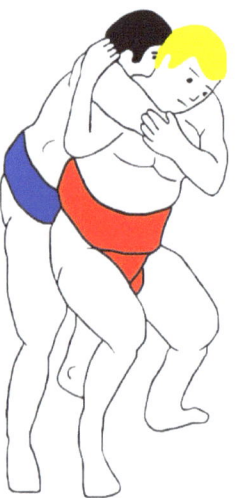

Step 2

Grab his arm with both hands and pull the arm forward while burying your hip under your opponent and heaving him over your shoulder.

Step 3

Throw your opponent over your shoulder by leaning forward and pulling him over your shoulder or hip.

IZORI

Backward Body Drop

Original 70: Yes

The attacker dives under his opponent's charge, grabs behind one or both knees or the front of the defender's mawashi, and uses his lower body or back to lift the opponent up and over backward. After draping opponent over the back and shoulders, fall backward so that opponent lands first.

IZORI

Backward Body Drop

Step 1

When your opponent leans over top of you, drop your hips to a very low crouch. When doing so, it is important that you place your head/neck in your opponent's armpit firmly.

Step 2

Once you have gripped your opponent's knee (best position) or his mawashi, begin to straighten your back and legs by standing and leaning backward and toward the side.

Step 3

Lift your opponent up and throw him down backward. The technique is executed by the spring/lift of your whole body at one time rather than by your hands, legs, hips, etc.

This technique is rarely seen and is very dangerous.

RARE

KAKEZORI

Leg Hook Backward Body Drop

Original 70: Yes

With his head under one of the defender's arms and an inside grip of his opponent's mawashi on the opposite side, the attacker attempts to twist the defender over or hook the defender's closest leg, driving his head into the defender's side to force him over backward.

KAKEZORI

Leg Hook Backward Body Drop

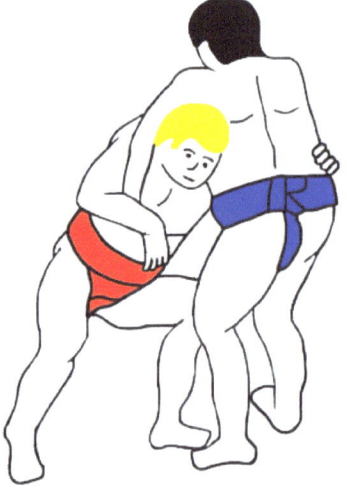

Step 1

After grabbing your opponent's inside gripping arm, drop your hips and drive your head under your opponent's armpit.

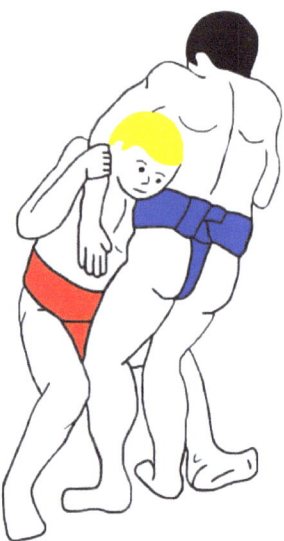

Step 2

With your opposite leg, hook your opponent's leg and/or twist him over.

Step 3

Lift your opponent and throw him over backward or toward the side.

RARE

OKURIGAKE

Rear Leg Trip

Original 70: No

From behind the defender, the attacker hooks one of his legs around one of the defender's legs, then pulls that hooked leg toward him, dropping his opponent forward and down.

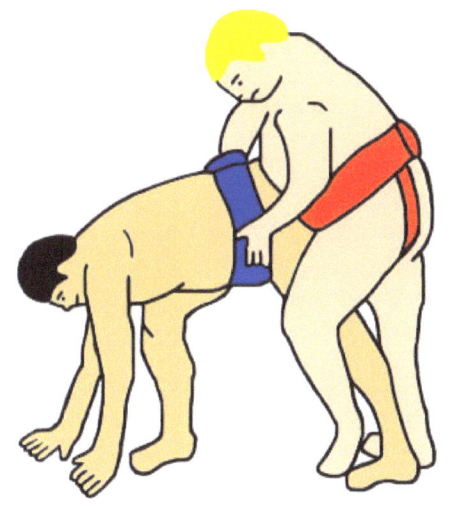

OKURIGAKE
Rear Leg Trip

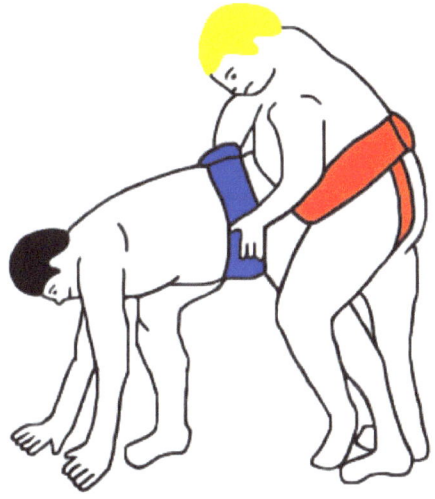

Step 1

After circling behind your opponent, hook your leg around one of his and force him to fall forward.

OKURITSURIOTOSHI

Rear Lift Body Slam

Original 70: No

After circling around behind the defender, the attacker lifts his opponent using any one of several possible grips and then slams him down.

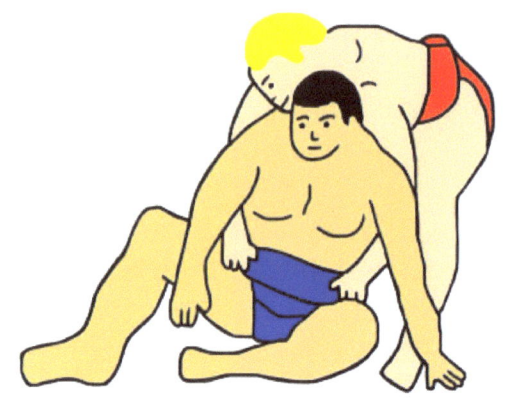

OKURITSURIOTOSHI
Rear Lift Body Slam

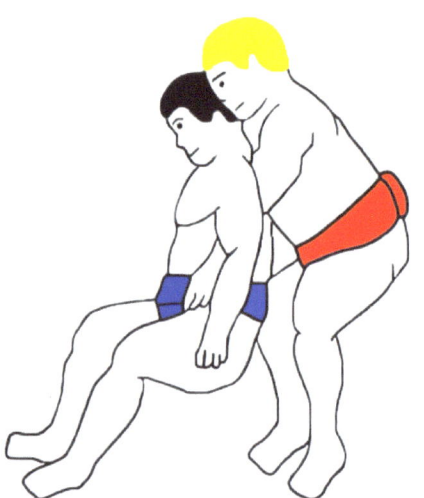

Step 1

After circling behind your opponent, lift him up and slam him down onto the dohyo without carrying him out of the ring.

RARE

SAKATOTTARI

Arm Bar Throw Counter

Original 70: Yes

Sakate means "reverse grip." A counter move to the tottari (arm bar throw), you free yourself from your opponent's arm bar and execute an arm bar throw on him by turning your hip closest to your opponent inward, forcing your opponent to fall forward.

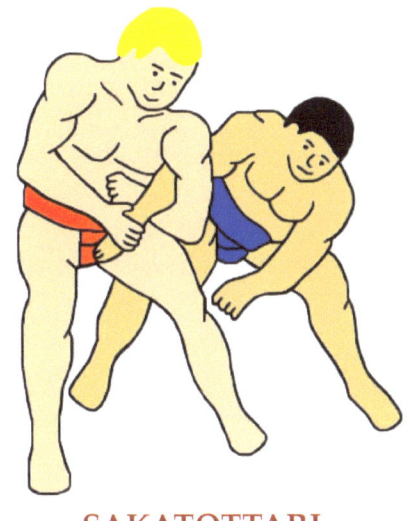

SAKATOTTARI
Arm Bar Throw Counter

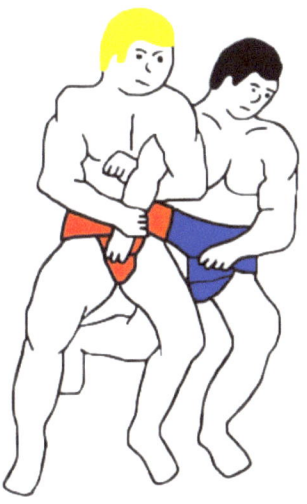

Step 1

When your opponent attempts tottari, free your arm by turning your hips and/or take a deep step forward with your lead leg quickly.

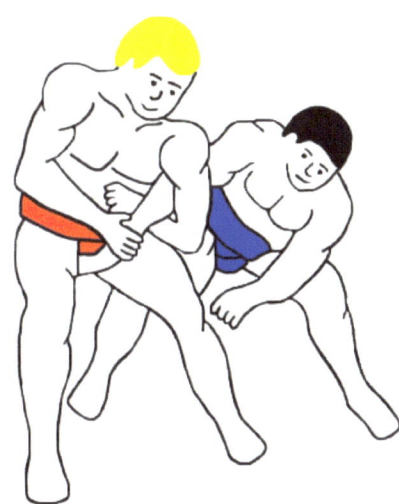

Step 2

Grab his arm, wrap and bar it, then twist.

Step 3

Force your opponent down by pulling downward on his arm.

RARE

SHUMOKUZORI

Bell Hammer Backward Body Drop

Original 70: Yes

The attacker ducks under the defender's lead arm and drapes the defender over the attacker's body in a fireman's carry position. The attacker then lifts the defender, taking him over backward. The attacker will land on his back an instant after the defender is thrown over onto his. *Shumoku* is a wooden bell hammer.

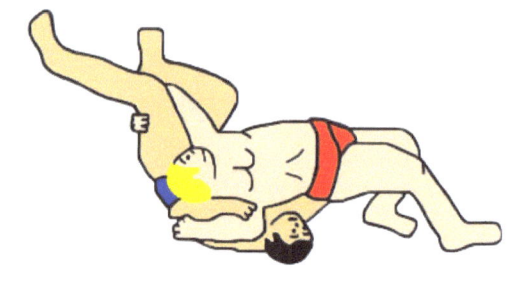

SHUMOKUZORI

Bell Hammer Backward Body Drop

This technique varies from Tasukizori in that one of your opponent's legs is still on the ground.

Step 1

When your opponent is over top of you from behind or the side, in somewhat of a fireman's carry, squat and grab his lead arm. Grab his leg with the other arm from an inside grip.

Step 2

Once you have gripped your opponent's leg, lift the leg, lean backward or twist toward the side.

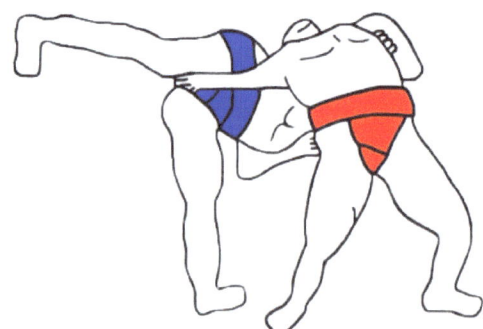

Step 3

Force your opponent to fall over onto his back by continuing to lean backward.

SOTOTASUKIZORI

Outside Reverse Backward Body Drop

Original 70: Yes

While the defender has an inside grip, the attacker bars that gripping arm across his own body, then reaches over that barred arm with his free hand palm up, grabbing the defender's closest leg from the inside at the thigh. Pulling the leg up and over forces the defender to touch the ground with his free hand.

SOTOTASUKIZORI

Outside Reverse Backward Body Drop

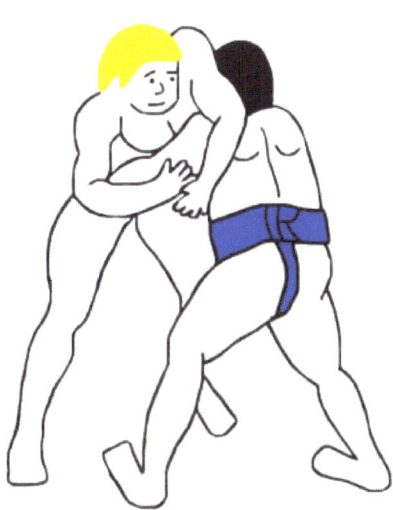

Step 1

When your opponent has an inside grip, lock that arm in place, and reach over him with your other arm so that you are on one side of his body, over his shoulder.

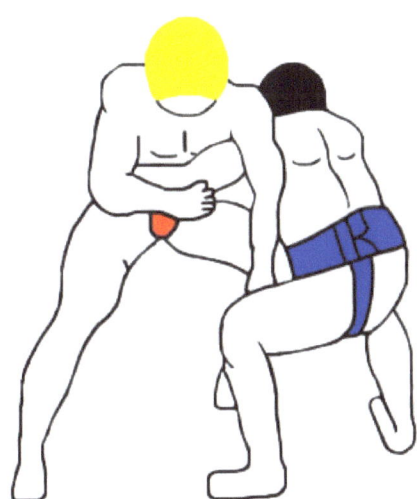

Step 2

While continuing to bar that arm with your one hand and body, grab your opponent's inner thigh, palm facing up.

Step 3

Keep your balance by squatting and lift your opponent's leg while leaning/twisting to the side and backward.

RARE

TASUKIZORI

Inside Reverse Backward Body Drop

Original 70: Yes

During a heated slapping exchange, the attacker ducks under the defender's lead arm with his back turned to the defender's side. Getting a hold on the defender's lead arm and his back leg at the thigh from the inside, the attacker then leans backward, driving the defender over onto his side or back.

This technique varies from Shumokuzori in that both of your opponent's legs are off the ground.

TASUKIZORI

Inside Reverse Backward Body Drop

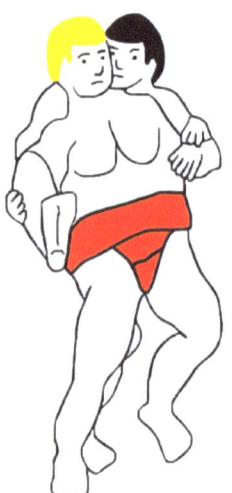

Step 1

When your opponent is over top of you from behind or the side, in somewhat of a fireman's carry, squat and grab his lead arm. Grab his leg with the other arm from an inside grip.

Step 2

Once you have gripped your opponent's leg, begin to straighten up and lean backward or twist toward the side.

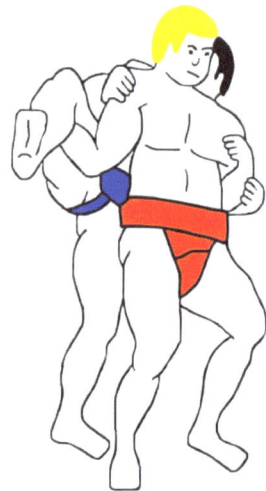

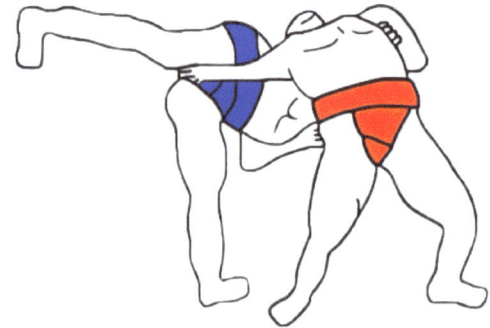

Step 3

Force your opponent to fall over onto his back by continuing to lean backward.

TOKKURINAGE

Two-Hand Head Twistdown

Original 70: No

The attacker takes advantage of the defender leaning forward, grabbing the opponent's head or neck with both hands to twist the defender down and over onto his back.

(*This technique was also called gasshohineri but that name is now used to describe a variation of tokkurinage.)

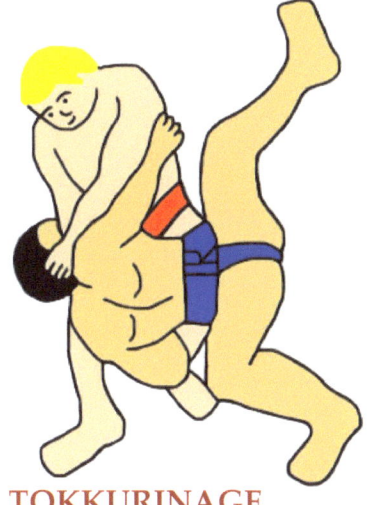

TOKKURINAGE

Two-Hand Head Twistdown

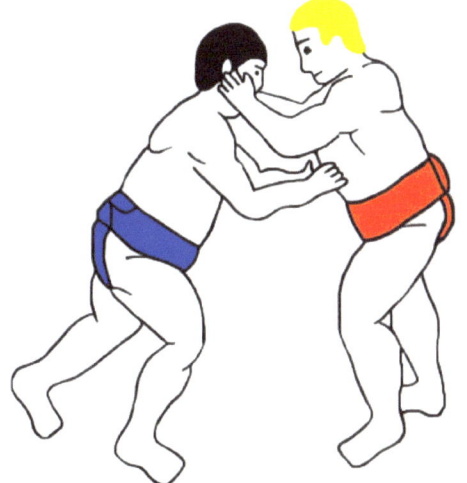

Step 1

Grab your opponent's head or neck with both hands.

(*If you clasp both hands together behind his head or neck, it would be gasshohineri.)

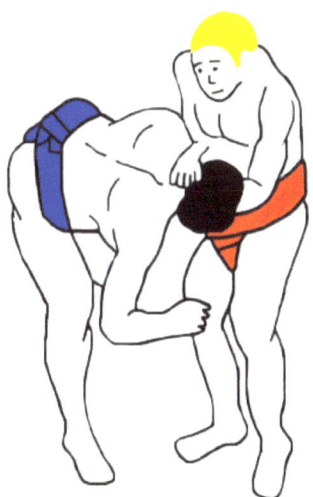

Step 2

Twist his head down to either the right or left.

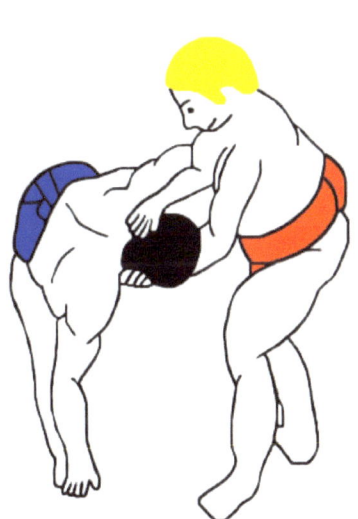

Step 3

This technique can be completed more effectively if you twist while throwing your opponent's head downward.

TSUMATORI

Rear Leg Pick

Original 70: Yes

The attacker must work his way to the side of his forward-moving opponent. As the defender lifts the foot closest to the attacker, the attacker reaches down, grabs that foot at the toes and pulls it back and up to forces his opponent to fall forward.

TSUMATORI

Rear Leg Pick

Step 1

From your inside grip position, maneuver to the side of your opponent. If your opponent gets an inside grip, you cannot complete this move until you release his inside grip.

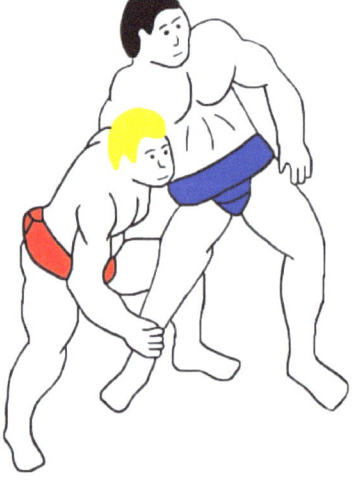

Step 2

Make your opponent lose his balance and trip forward. Get your shoulder under his armpit and grab his ankle.

Step 3

Lift your opponent's leg up and back to force him to fall forward. When this technique is done successfully, your opponent will touch the dohyo with both hands while tripping forward.

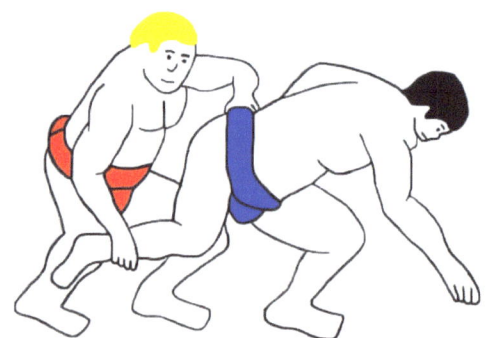

RARE

TSUTAEZORI

Underarm Forward Body Drop

Original 70: No

The attacker dives under one of the defender's arms while maintaining a grip on that arm. Leaning back and into the defender, he forces him to fall forward and touch down with his free hand.

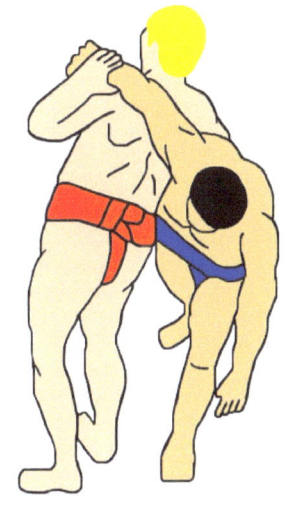

TSUTAEZORI

Underarm Forward Body Drop

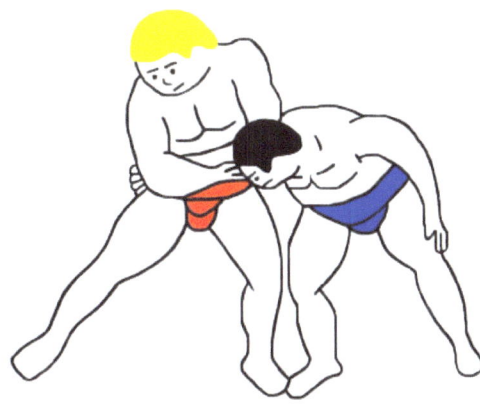

Step 1

When your opponent attempts to take an inside grip, grab his wrist and dive under his arm.

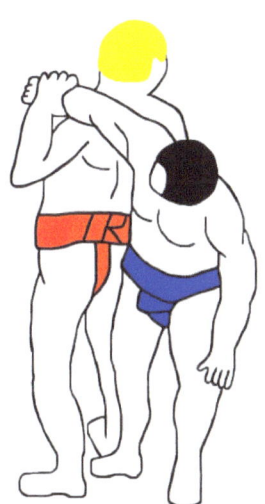

Step 2

Continue to pull that arm to keep your opponent off balance while turning away from him.

Step 3

Lean back into your opponent and force him to fall down or touch with his other hand.

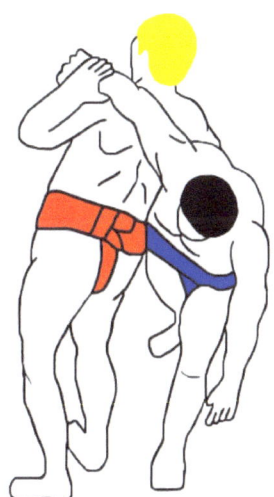

BIBLIOGRAPHY

Material

Shimokawa, T. *et al.* (2002). *Sumo.* Tokyo: Hiraka Manufacturing Co.
Illustrations by: Kurata, H. and Watanabe, K.
ISBN: 4-900428-37-X

Hikoyama, K. (1940). *SUMO – Japanese Wrestling.* Tokyo: Maruzen Co Ltd.
ISBN: 286 L 34-2040

Newton, C. (1994). *Dynamic Sumo.* Tokyo: Kodansha International Ltd.
ISBN: 4-7700-1802-9

Kuhaulua, J. and Wheeler, J. (1973). *TAKAMIYAMA The World of Sumo.* Tokyo: Kodansha International Ltd.

Unknown, (n.d.), *IFS*, Retrieved June 19, 2005, from International Sumo Federation website: http://amateursumo.com/ifs.htm

Unknown, (n.d.), *Sumo*, Retrieved June 19, 2005, from International Sumo Federation website: http://amateursumo.com/sumo.htm

Illustrations

Illustrations by: Keller, Maggie and Zabel, Thomas, 2012/2013

Shimokawa, T. *et al.* (2002). *Sumo.* Tokyo: Hiraka Manufacturing Co.
Illustrations by: Kurata, H. and Watanabe, K.
ISBN: 4-900428-37-X

Unknown. (n.d.), *Sumo Techniques*, Retrieved June 19, 2005, from Japan Times Online website: http//www.japantimes.co.jp/sports/sumo_techniques.html